SCOTTISH WRITERS

Editor
DAVID DAICHES

GEORGE MacDONALD

DAVID S. ROBB

SCOTTISH ACADEMIC PRESS

EDINBURGH

Published by
Scottish Academic Press Ltd.
33 Montgomery Street, Edinburgh EH7 5JX

First published 1987
SBN 7073 0523 3

© 1987 Text and Bibliography
David S. Robb

British Library Cataloguing in Publication Data
Robb, David S.
    George MacDonald.—(Scottish writers: 11).
    1. MacDonald, George, 1824–1905—
    Criticism and interpretation
    I. Title   II. Series
    823'.8   PR4969

    ISBN 0-7073-0523-3

Printed in Great Britain by
Bell and Bain Ltd, Glasgow

CONTENTS

ABBREVIATIONS

The following abbreviations of the titles of MacDonald's publications are used.

The following refer to the single-volume reprint editions which are the usual form in which MacDonald's novels are available.

AF   *Alec Forbes of Howglen*
CW   *Castle Warlock*
DE   *David Elginbrod*
M   *Malcolm*
Ph   *Phantastes*
RF   *Robert Falconer*
WC   *Wilfred Cumbermede*

The following specific editions are also used.

ABNW   *At the Back of the North Wind*, New York, 1950.
P&C   *The Princess and Curdie*, Harmondsworth, 1966.
P&G   *The Princess and the Goblin*, Harmondsworth, 1964.
US   *Unspoken Sermons, Series One*, London, 1867.

CHAPTER 1

LIFE AND WORK

George MacDonald was born in Huntly, in Aberdeenshire, in 1824. He was the second eldest of a family of six boys, of whom four survived into manhood. When he was eight, his mother died: Robert Lee Wolff has argued that MacDonald never fully recovered from the trauma of his mother's early death.[1] Seven years after her death, his father married again and three girls were added to the family, though by the time they began to appear George had essentially left the family home to be a student in Aberdeen. Even as a child, his health was somewhat weak, though he was able to participate fully in the open-air life of a country boy. Although born in Huntly itself, MacDonald from the age of two was brought up on the nearby farm which George MacDonald Snr worked jointly with his brother James. The MacDonalds were a notably religious family, being prominent in the life of an independent chapel called the Missionar Kirk.

Huntly is set in the heart of rural Aberdeenshire and was the centre for the life and produce of a lowland economy in which the land was farmed in a modern, efficient way. On the other hand, Huntly also nestles in the lee of the eastern highlands of Scotland; the hills meant not only a bleaker physical environment and a harsher economic struggle for their inhabitants, but created a cultural and linguistic difference, as well. Young George would have been familiar with the sound of Gaelic, even though his own languages were the Aberdeenshire Scots which was the speech of his street games, and the English, heavily coloured by Aberdeenshire inflections, no doubt, which was insisted upon at formal family occasions. To the north was the Moray Firth coast, a region to which the inhabitants of the Aberdeenshire hinterland resorted for holidays, and to drink sea-water for medicinal purposes. From here, too, fisher-wives tramped with huge baskets of freshly-caught fish on their backs, to sell to the farmers and the inland townspeople. During George's boyhood, the possibility of change in the leasing of farms was ever-present, but it was not until 1841 that a new system was adopted whereby groups of small farms were grouped into one large unit — a step that had been resisted by an older generation of the local landowners, the Dukes of Gordon, out of a sense of loyalty to families with long associations with particular farms. At about the same time, the town was also suffering economically due to the decline in the lint industry, thanks to cheaper lint from Holland and then to the arrival of the even cheaper cotton. A surprising amount of all this found its way into George MacDonald's fiction many years later.

The North-East is a part of Scotland which has not only tended to retain the distinctiveness of its regional identity through many centuries and through many changes, but it has fostered a marked and sturdy independence in its inhabitants. One seemingly superficial but important indicator of this regional individualism is the extraordinary distinctiveness of its vernacular, while another is the vitality, even today, of its oral tradition of ballad and folk-song. In religion, too, the North-East has usually gone its own way, and for centuries after the Reformation both Episcopalianism and Romanism survived the Presbyterian onslaught with greater tenacity there than in any other important part of lowland Scotland.

Observable facts such as these are only the outward

manifestations of an individualism in everyday life which is easier to assert than to illustrate. One notes, however, that L. J. Saunders, still probably the best historian of the Scotland of MacDonald's youth, regularly touches on the spirit of self-reliance as a key feature of the area, in such matters as organised poor relief, for example.[2] This is corroborated by a Huntly man, George Gray, reminiscing in 1892 in his *Recollections of Huntly as it was Seventy Years Ago*, and stating it as his belief that more was given to the poor when relief was voluntary than after it was made compulsory: his preference for seeing alms-giving as a moral duty rather than as a legal one is especially interesting in the light of the later portions of *Robert Falconer*, for example.[3] Another voice of the people of the Victorian North-East, Christian Watt of Fraserburgh, articulates an independence of attitude which, while markedly her own, is also clearly characteristic of the community which moulded her, as when she marvels at the docility of the Highlanders in the face of clearance.[4]

In this land of independent spirits, the MacDonalds of Huntly were particularly noted for their enterprise. George Gray's account mentions them several times, and brings out their prominence in the community to a degree which the author's son Greville MacDonald, for all the adoration with which he writes of his father and grandfather in his biography, fails to convey. Gray tells us that the MacDonald brothers (that is, George's father and uncles) 'belonged to the most enterprising family then in the place'. Their energy was particularly noteworthy at the farm of Upper Pirriesmill 'which at this time came into the possession of Messrs George and James Macdonald [sic], who, within a few years, reclaimed more land in proportion to the extent of the holding than any other tenant in the district'.[5] The energy of this particular family, furthermore, was partly representative of the dynamism of their religious

community, the Missionar Kirk. Describing the
Missionars, Gray sums up part of the world of *Alec
Forbes*, for, he says, they

> ...comprised the most energetic men in the
> locality — men remarkable alike for religious zeal
> and activity in business... They were ultra-
> Sabbatarian; so much so that the sending out of a
> bairn to fetch milk on Sunday morning was
> condemned as wrong. And while Sunday walking
> may have been disapproved of by other Churches,
> among the *Missionars* it was absolutely condemned
> and reprobated... Moreover, the free use of
> intoxicants, although it may have been tolerated or
> winked at in some of the other congregations, met
> here with unqualified reprobation. They were also
> very exclusive in regard to membership.[6]

A marked energy in the affairs of both this world and
the other world — the dual commitment which we find
in the thought and writing of the most famous of these
MacDonalds — was clearly 'a family (and
denominational) feature. It is perhaps summed up
nowhere more strikingly than in the person of
MacDonald's grandmother, who burned the sinful
fiddle of her son Charles, thereby providing her
grandson with the most memorable episode in one of
his best novels, *Robert Falconer* (1867), but who also
exhibited a marked commercial practicality, as
Greville's account makes clear:

> The good lady, though stuff of the old
> Covenanting martyrs, had as fine an instinct for
> the righteous care of the valuables deposited with
> her husband, the banker — so he was called — as
> she had for the salvation of souls... The bank had
> not even a safe until Mrs. Charles Edward
> appropriated to this use the family *Chanter Kist*, the
> traditional receptacle of family records.[7]

Two worlds, then, came together in MacDonald's family experience; from an early age he was being shown the possibility of reconciling them, although how precarious the balance could be was brought forcibly home to the MacDonalds at least once when his uncle Charles fell imprudently into debt and absconded to America, leaving his brothers, James and George (the novelist's father) to carry moral responsibility for repayment.

The Missionars were distinct in other ways, too: for example, Gray tells us that 'a school was taught by the late Mr. William Spence, in a disused weaver's shop, upon the feu now occupied by the Free Church. Most of the scholars belonged to the *Missionar* congregation'.[8] Who exactly were these Missionars amongst whom the future religious novelist grew up? The Missionar Kirk in Huntly was originally an Anti-burgher Secession church — that is to say, it was a product of the secession from the established Kirk of Scotland by the Erskine brothers and their adherents in 1733, and of the later sub-dividing of that original secession into those ministers who agreed, or refused, to take an oath, called the burgess oath, which could be interpreted as an approval of the established church. At first glance, these eighteenth-century squabbles seem to have more to do with church government than with doctrine, but in fact the real issue was between different concepts of what religion was and should be in the Age of Reason. For most of the eighteenth century and well into the nineteenth, the dominant grouping among the ministers and elders of the Kirk was known as the Moderates. By and large, these men had a vision of the religious life which harmonised with the developments in culture, politeness and knowledge which we now call the Scottish Enlightenment. Such men turned their backs thankfully on the enthusiasm, the irrationality, and the violence of thought, language and deed which were the hallmarks of seventeenth-century religious life. The Moderates essentially despised their Evangelical opponents as foolish fanatics. The Evangelicals, in their turn, regarded the Moderates as worldly compromisers, traitors to their national religious inheritance and to religion itself. In a sense, the Evangelicals were the heirs of the Covenanters, and however much we may now feel more comfortable with the prevailing Moderatism, it has to be recognised that it must have lacked some essential religious ingredient, in view of the spontaneous and independent growths of revivalism which became common in the later part of the eighteenth century and the first half of the nineteenth. It was this revivalist spirit which eventually overtook the Kirk in the form of the Disruption of 1843 and the creation of the Free Kirk of Scotland, but all denominations were liable to give rise to movements of revival at this time.

MacDonald's immediate religious inheritance, therefore, was deeply and characteristically Scottish. It was not primarily the element of hell-fire, however, which made it so; rather, its Scottishness was due to the independent, democratic insistence on a non-pragmatic, idealistic faith, fiercely felt within the individual. Despite his subsequent rejection of some of his theological inheritance, MacDonald's spirit always had the combativeness, the stiff-neckedness, the absoluteness of the Covenanters whose distant heir he was. He was one of Scotland's many religious outsiders, though more attractive, now, perhaps, than most of them.

The Huntly Missionars not only passed that tradition on to him, however; they considerably intensified it, for they were rebels even within their own rebellious Antiburgher minority. Amongst the most prominent of the revivalists who appeared during the spiritual upsurge in Britain towards the end of the eighteenth century were the two Haldane brothers, who were viewed with suspicion by most ministers in all denominations because they were laymen who dared to preach. During their tour of Britain in 1797, however, James Haldane was allowed, by the minister of the Huntly Anti-burgher chapel, George Cowie, to preach there, a fault Cowie repeated for another evangelist two years later — and he listened to them himself. For these transgressions, Cowie was excommunicated. Despite this, his Huntly flock grew. After his death in 1806, they had no settled minister for another ten years, but during that time the Huntly Missionars drifted into the ambit of the spreading Congregational denomination.[9]

To outsiders, the difference between Congregationalism and the Presbyterianism of the established Kirk must have seemed minimal, especially as their theologies were not notably different. Yet, in the first half of the nineteenth century, the difference in spirit between the two seems to have been very great. Congregationalism was the outcome of powerful and fresh revivalist feelings, and its stress on matters of church government was related to fervent ideals of what a church community should be, with a lively spirit of fellowship, a strong sense of the duty of members to watch over and help each other, and a scrupulousness as to the beliefs and conduct of all its members. Furthermore, the Congregationalists' urge to spread the Evangel was strong — hence, the interest in both overseas and home missions — and their leaders were notable for being aggressively outspoken. Thus, MacDonald's response to his religious background was not merely one of rejecting hell-fire theology, nor his willingness to be an outsider. From it, he was able to draw positive things such as his fervent outreach to all men, the evangelistic spirit in which he wrote, and his sense of the ideal Christian community — small, organically alive, looking back to the early days of Christianity, as in the circle which grows round Robert Falconer, or the patriarchal, clan groupings of the Portlossie novels (*Malcolm* and *The Marquis of Lossie*) and *What's Mine's Mine*. The religion of his youth was one of the most positive formative influences on his life and work, and it was guiding and moulding him long after he left Huntly in 1840 to study at one of Aberdeen's two universities, King's College in Old Aberdeen, where his adult life began.

His first major prose work, *Phantastes*, tells of how Anodos (often translated as 'the pathless one') wanders through a world which may be a dream. In one of his later Scottish novels, he makes his hero look back on his varied fortunes and experiences and exclaim, 'It's like going on and on in a dream, wondering what's coming next!' (CW, p. 303; Chap. 53, 'Help').[10] That human life is dream-like is an idea which seems to have occurred often to the creator of Cosmo Warlock and the heavy-eyed Anodos. MacDonald's adult life lacked the clear direction and controlled predictability that some are given to experience. Instead, it was a tale of changing intentions and unexpected difficulties; projected careers had, perforce, to give place to unlooked-for alternatives. What he did, where he lived, how he was to support his many dependents — all these were continually being discovered anew throughout his long career. He and his family lived a hand-to-mouth existence: even as late as 1887 he was writing to a friend, 'Once again I come a beggar to your door for my big handful of meal! Could you let us have your usual kind gift this year. I should gladly pay for it but the offer to do so has become such a form by your always refusing to accept it, that it comes easier to beg for it right out'.[11] Yet his later years were spent as master of a large house in the northern Italian coastal town of Bordighera; this was acquired largely with generous donations from friends and well-wishers. In 1900, MacDonald and his wife were installed in a house, specially designed for them, in Haslemere. It had 'lovely gardens and three acres of woodland with superb beeches that overspread the road' (GMDW, p. 560). More than for most of us, life was given to MacDonald rather than taken by him. It was an experience which needed, but also gave rise to, faith.

As students in all times and places find, MacDonald discovered that the move to university brought him a host of new experiences. Much of the work was new to the product of a rural 'adventure' school where the curriculum would not have extended much beyond reading, writing, arithmetic — and the Latin which constituted the rite of passage, via the annual open competition for King's College's many bursaries, to the world of more advanced learning. MacDonald took the four-year course leading to the Master of Arts degree which in Scotland, then as now, stressed breadth and variety. The course for the four years' study leading to the M.A. degree had, at its core, Greek (three hours a day) and Latin (one hour, or a little more, per day). Study of these two subjects was maintained throughout the course with, in addition, Mathematics, Physics (or 'Natural Philosophy' as it is called at Aberdeen) and, in the final year, Logic and Moral Philosophy. This last, despite its bias towards Scottish Common Sense, contained material which MacDonald clearly responded to, including 'the philosophy of Bacon as applied to the science of mind' and 'the doctrines of Natural Theology and the Immortality of the Soul'.[12] Furthermore, the Aberdeen Arts students had to do a year of Chemistry, taken in any year but the first. This compulsion had been an idiosyncracy of the course at King's for some time, but in the earlier years of the century had been taught amateurishly by various professors, of Maths, Philosophy or Latin. From 1840, however, the class was taught by William Gregory, the Professor of Medicine, last of the famous Gregory family of Scottish academics and the first chemist of real stature to teach at King's College.[13]

There was novelty, too, in the life of a large city during a time of social and economic upheaval. Greville MacDonald twice touches on the great Chartist demonstration of 29 October 1841 at which Fergus O'Connor, newly released from prison, was marched through the city at the head of a huge carnival procession of the Aberdeen trades. The day culminated in a half-hour speech from O'Connor to a crowd of five thousand: 'The scene was really splendid', wrote George in a letter to his father (GMDW, p. 69). According to a recent historian, this day initiated in earnest the Chartist movement in the city.[14] In the 1830s there had been very little popular radicalism in the city, but several years of increasing economic depression had transformed this situation. At first, different trades were hit unequally, but among the first to feel the squeeze were the shoemakers and the tailors, from whose ranks, consequently, many of the leading Aberdeen Chartists emerged. (In his later writing, it is often in one or other of these trades that MacDonald locates his independent-minded and outspoken artisan spokesmen.) The Aberdeen of his student days provided MacDonald with his first detailed knowledge of Victorian urban squalor.

It was while a student at Aberdeen, too, that MacDonald encountered several of the many reverses of his adult life, although there have been ascribed to this period yet further troubles which may be mere fiction. In his book, *The Golden Key*, Robert Lee Wolff makes his famous claim that, in 1842, during a vacation job cataloguing a private library in a castle in the north of Scotland, MacDonald had an emotionally wounding romance with a thoughtlessly teasing upper-class girl.[15] The evidence for this lies in the frequent appearance of this situation in his writing rather than in any documentary evidence, and there are those who discount the theory. It is at least a possibility, however, and seems to me more likely than another inference about his student days which is current, namely that he indulged in drink and prostitutes.[16] This assumption seems to be based on the behaviour of Alec Forbes, who temporarily goes to the dogs in the course of a novel which admittedly has a strong autobiographical basis. This hardly seems sufficient evidence upon which to base such a serious charge, especially when it is unsupported by anything we can gather about the circles in which MacDonald moved when he was not studying. Nevertheless, these youthful days in Aberdeen had their difficulties and disasters.

While a student, George MacDonald lodged with his brother Charles in the home of one Peter Taylor, who was a prominent deacon in the Congregational church, Blackfriars Street Chapel, which the MacDonalds attended.[17] Taylor's strictness — the blinds were drawn from Saturday night until Monday morning — was typical of the denomination, which even by the standards of the day had a narrow code of conduct and discipline. A book of minutes, recording church meetings from 2 October 1844 onwards, has been preserved and shows how regularly the congregation was called upon to discipline (which often meant expelling) erring members of the flock.[18] The minister at Blackfriars Street, however, was no mere unenlightened bigot; he was a youthful, energetic man with a powerful social conscience and a gift for preaching which drew the young in particular to his feet. Dr. John Kennedy was one of Aberdeen's leading churchmen and Greville MacDonald makes clear how his father received much help and support from him. At one point, however, MacDonald and his minister were severely at odds. As part of their outreach to the citizens of Aberdeen, the Blackfriars Street congregation had established a Sunday School in the Town Hall of Old Aberdeen, beside King's College. During the university sessions, the regular staff of this offshoot had the help of students, of whom George MacDonald was one.[19] The Sunday School staff became fired, however, with the doctrines of the Rev. James Morison, an Independent minister who, on taking up the charge of the obscure community of the Cabrach in 1839, had started a lively religious revival with his fervent preaching of Universalist doctrine. Morison was swiftly disowned by his own denomination and those who hearkened to him tended to suffer similar fates, be they individuals or entire church communities. Morisonianism was a prime cause of schism in the world of the Scottish Independent churches of the 1840s, and it is to this controversy that Greville MacDonald refers when he tells how 'the offer of release from some of their mental chains took strong hold of certain young men attached to the Blackfriars Congregational Church in Aberdeen, greatly to Dr. Kennedy's concern. Among these black sheep most certainly was George MacDonald' (GMDW, p. 79). What Greville does not make clear is that the entire regular teaching staff was summarily dismissed and, despite the appointment of a fresh and doctrinally sound team, the Sunday School was soon defunct. So severe was the controversy within the Blackfriars community that soon afterwards the church itself split and a breakaway church was established in nearby St. Paul Street, though that occurred in 1846 after MacDonald left Aberdeen. What Greville MacDonald touches on as a mild peccadillo was in fact, for his father, an early direct taste of the ferocity with which Victorian religious controversy was waged. When, in the 1850s, MacDonald became a more prominent participant in such warfare, he was already battle-hardened.

We can find out a certain amount about the church

environment which MacDonald inhabited while a student. What we cannot chart in detail is the development of his characteristic theological views. Greville suggests that a letter of 5 January 1841 indicates that his father was not, at that point, questioning the traditional dogmas: 'I hope I wish to serve God and to be delivered not only from the punishment of sin, but also from its power' (GMDW, p. 68). By the time that he took over the Congregational church in Arundel in 1850, he appears to have been in the Universalist camp. I think it safe to assume that it was during his undergraduate days at Aberdeen that his rejection of traditional Calvinist doctrines began in earnest. Greville clearly implies that it was an unsettling time of some real unhappiness, and rightly points to the autobiographical element in the poem *The Disciple* with its picture of a student disturbed by the unacceptable face of God:

> They preach men should not faint, but pray,
>   And seek until they find;
> But God is very far away,
>   Nor is his countenance kind.[20]

And just as his religious life was proving to have its pitfalls and surprises, so his progress to life's other goals also proved far from straightforward. From Greville's account, it seems more than likely that his father fell in love with 'his beautiful and accomplished cousin Helen MacKay' (GMDW, pp. 82–83). Indeed, it seems possible that it was MacDonald's failure to secure her rather than any putative library flirt which lies behind all those unhappy love affairs in his fiction. At the same time, MacDonald was finding that financial difficulties were standing in his way. It is for this reason that Greville explains his father's missing of the session 1842–43, although those who suspect MacDonald of student debauchery suggest that the absence had something to do with his falling off. There seems little reason to doubt Greville, however, when he says that shortage of family funds prevented his father from following his impulses to do advanced work in chemistry and then, as an alternative, to switch to medicine (GMDW, p. 68).

The choice of these two possible careers undoubtedly reflects aspects of MacDonald's mental and moral outlook. The fact, however, that, at King's in the early 1840s, they were both associated with one man holds out the further possibility that the undergraduate had to some extent fallen under the spell of a particularly effective teacher. To the best of my knowledge, MacDonald mentions William Gregory in his published writing only once when, in *Castle Warlock*, he makes his young student hero contemplate going 'to Germany to Liebig, or to Edinburgh to Gregory' (CW, p. 170; chap. 26, 'At College'). (Gregory moved to Edinburgh in late 1844 to occupy the chair of Chemistry there, a position he held until his death in 1858.) Gregory was a pupil and disciple of Liebig's, whose work he introduced to Britain in the 1840s. Liebig had developed the study of organic chemistry, so that his laboratory at Giessen was where the frontiers of the subject were to be found. Even as late as 1850, the lure of working with Liebig was strong enough to seem to MacDonald a real alternative even to entering the ministry (GMDW, p. 70).

The contact with Gregory appeared to hold out, for some considerable time, the possibility of a career in either medicine or chemistry; Gregory's emphasis on organic chemistry must have seemed to mean working at the point where life and matter met. Furthermore, I think it more than likely that it was Gregory who, more than anyone, opened MacDonald's eyes to another of life's possibilities. While he was at Aberdeen, Gregory began to dabble in spiritualism, or animal magnetism as it was then called. It was a spare time occupation, of course, but he experimented with hypnotism and read widely in the field as a whole. Eventually, he published his findings in his *Letters to a Candid Inquirer on Animal Magnetism* (1851) and in a pamphlet of 1852.[21] It appears that he would occasionally enlist the cooperation of students, both in Aberdeen and Edinburgh, in his experiments. We cannot assume that MacDonald was one of those involved but it seems possible that he knew of Gregory's preoccupation. It is clear that the author of *David Elginbrod* had a very considerable knowledge of, and interest in, animal magnetism and indeed, his writing throughout his career betrays an awareness of magnetic lore.

Graduation in 1845 forced him to grapple with the problems of this world, however, and his first employment was as tutor to a non-conformist family in Fulham. He hated this, partly because the children he taught were little brats, but the tutorship could never have been regarded as other than a stop-gap. It was not until 1848, however, that he relinquished it so that he could train as a Congregational minister. In the meantime, he had met the girl whom he would marry, Louisa Powell. At last, the doubts about his way ahead seemed to have been resolved, especially when he received a call to the Congregational pulpit at Arundel in 1850. In November of that year, however, he was laid low by a severe haemorrhage of blood from the lungs. While a child, he had been less sturdy than other boys, but it was this attack at the outset of his adult career which marked the entrance into his life of a factor which would play a major part in its shaping. The constant danger to his lungs forced him to spend many winters by the Mediterranean, a necessity which greatly exacerbated his never-ending financial problems and meant that he and his large family had to regularly move their entire establishment from one end of Europe to the other. They had constantly to rely on the generosity of others to make all this possible; Byron's widow, who funded the first of those winter migrations (to Algiers in 1856), was only the first of many well-wishers willing to pay to help keep MacDonald alive. The need to subsidise these travels led, in turn, to other journeys: MacDonald undertook an arduous lecture-tour of the U.S.A. in 1872–73, and until very late in life, he participated in the family's theatrical productions (which included Shakespeare as well as Mrs. MacDonald's dramatisation of *The Pilgrim's Progress*) with which they toured Britain in an attempt to supplement their income. Even as late as 1885, he was writing to a friend: 'We were four months in Scotland, and were very kindly received — with our Pilgrims. Though we cannot say we made any money exactly, we kept ourselves, and that is much, for it is the daily bread'.[22] MacDonald's affliction must have contributed substantially to his sense of being a mere transient pilgrim in this world and of the world itself being less than the ultimate reality. Thanks to it, he was hindered from feeling rooted in any one place: much of the story that Greville tells is of moves from one house to another, with, on each occasion, the fresh start at making a home. The house in Bordighera, Casa Coraggio, was perhaps the nearest to a permanent home that they knew, but even it had to be left each year for the return to Britain. Nor could MacDonald ever have felt that sense of establishment which comes with financial security. Even less could he have ever been long free from the knowledge of human mortality and transcience: not only was his own death an ever-present possibility, but he had to bear the loss of many of those dearest to him, from his father and brothers in the 1850s to four of his children and a grandchild (and his wife in 1902) in later years. MacDonald's experience must have encouraged him to feel the power of the verse: 'For we are strangers before thee, and sojourners, as were all our fathers: our days on the earth are as a shadow, and there is none abiding' (I Chronicles 29. 15).

None of this could have been foreseen as MacDonald, recovered from the attack of November 1850, married and took up his responsibilities as a minister. Yet within three years he had parted from the Arundel congregation and was struggling to make ends meet to support his growing family. Whether the relinquishment of his pulpit came about because of the refusal of a narrow-minded church community to accept the theological sophistication of their eager and uncompromising young pastor, as Greville suggests (GMDW, pp. 177–87), or whether, as Muriel Hutton has argued,[23] MacDonald rapidly felt constricted by the life he had chosen and broke out so as to devote himself to literature, the end result was that he moved to Manchester in 1853, where his brother Charles lived and also where A. J. Scott, the first principal of Owen's College and a sharer in MacDonald's religious opinions, was to be found. MacDonald lived there for two and a half years, setting up his own preaching room, giving lectures on English literature and on science, and writing.

From this point on, the remainder of MacDonald's long life is a tale of many homes, much travelling, constant care for his own health, regular sadness for the deaths of others, never-ending dependence on the financial help of friends and well-wishers (despite the ingenious ploys of his family in supplementing the family income, and despite the occasional salaried appointment) and ceaseless writing. In the 1860s and 1870s, he became extremely well-known as a novelist, with a reputation for work which was notably intellectual and high-minded. For a few years, from

1869, he edited a periodical with the self-explanatory title of *Good Words for the Young*, for which he produced several of his major works for children. Fame and esteem, from both sides of the Atlantic, were his, but they never became translated into financial independence, though such factors as his eleven children, and the pirating of successful British books by unscrupulous American publishers (so that American royalties were not forthcoming), contributed to the discrepancy. In his own day, however, it was felt that his place was among the prominent writers of the age, with many of whom he was acquainted. Among his intimate friends he could count Charles Kingsley, Charles Dodgson and John Ruskin. A long literary career can be hard to sustain, however, and in MacDonald's case the novelist whose works struck a chord with the readers of the 1860s and 1870s looked increasingly anachronistic and out of tune with taste in the 1880s and 1890s. In this world of shadows, literary taste and reputation are among life's shifting realities. He died in 1905.

MacDonald's first attempts at writing were poems, and the long poem *Within and Without* was his first original published work. He always preferred poetry to prose, as his son Ronald testifies, and he thought of himself as a poet first and foremost.[24] He regularly contributed verse to such publications as *Good Words* and *The Sunday Magazine*. Few of his novels, too, lack verse, which he worked in when he could. His collected poems fill two volumes, although even they do not contain everything he wrote. His poetry is disappointing. It is often clumsy in sound, rhythm and phrasing: too often, the effect is of ideas versified, rather than of a conception in which sound and idea are unified. It is interesting that this is not so true of his poems in Scots, where the rhythms become firmer, clearer, and more musical.

He was also a translator and editor. His translation

of some of the *Spiritual Songs* of Novalis was one of the things held against him by his Arundel flock, and in later years he published two further volumes of verse translation, mainly from the German. Several times he, in his own word, 'presented' (rather than 'edited') the works of earlier writers, producing editions and anthologies which laid as much emphasis on his own personality and views as they do on the texts themselves; these last were offered to view through the prominent medium of MacDonald's own sense of them. This is a pattern we find in nearly everything he wrote. In 1874, for example, he published *England's Antiphon*, an anthology of religious poems set in a continuous discursive narrative: it is an extended lecture in book form on the history of English religious poetry and is notable for its high appreciation of Donne. In 1885, he published an edition of *Hamlet* in which each page of text is opposed by a page of interpretative and critical notes which, taken together, consitute a vivid and passionate interpretation. This is one of MacDonald's more eccentric productions: one feels that Hamlet is being transformed into one of his own fictional Christian heroes. Yet another favourite author, Sidney, was 'presented' in 1891 in *A Cabinet of Gems*, while a readership was even more directly addressed in the three volumes of *Unspoken Sermons* (1867–89), and in the collection of essays entitled *Orts* (1882) or *A Dish of Orts* (1893), mainly on literary and personal topics.

The great bulk of MacDonald's writing is fiction, and although I think that the differences between the main types of his fiction are far less important or real than is usually assumed, classification makes description of his output easier. Most of his books are what we must loosely call 'realistic novels', meaning that they purport to be set in our everyday world. However improbable characters, speech and actions may be, they give us a version of the world with which we are familiar. Many of them are set in places with which we know MacDonald was acquainted and a dozen are set wholly or in large part in Scotland. We may call these the Scottish novels, and the remainder the English novels. Both types were produced at all stages of his career: at no period does one predominate over the other. The realistic fiction includes short stories such as those in *The Gifts of the Child Christ and other tales* (1882), and some works for children such as *Ranald Bannerman's Boyhood* (1871) and *Gutta Percha Willie* (1873).

We may use the term fantasy to cover most of the rest of MacDonald's fiction. By this term, I mean works set wholly or partly in a domain which is other than the everyday world, or works containing characters or elements clearly lying outside normal human experience, such as North Wind, or the supernatural in *The Portent*. Of the works of this type, several are clearly intended for adults, such as *Phantastes* (1858) and *Lilith* (1895), while others are definitely written for children although they can also appeal to adults. These include *At the Back of the North Wind* (1870, 1871), *The Princess and the Goblin* (1871, 1872) and *The Princess and Curdie* (1882, 1883). Much of MacDonald's fantasy writing is in short-story form, and was published in periodicals, interpolated into longer works, or appeared in collections such as *Dealings with the Fairies* (1867) and *The Light Princess and other fairy stories* (1890).

Obviously, this variety of forms elicited from MacDonald a corresponding variety of styles and tones in his writing. Nevertheless, it is possible to generalise about what we encounter, in terms of orientation, ideas and personality, in this vast quantity of material. Everything he wrote was filled with his sense of God, and with what he believed to be the truth about God and God's Creation. He could not help giving expression to a conception of reality which far transcends what he often referred to as the commonplace world. It is true his son Ronald, asking his father if he would not have liked to have written 'a story of mere human passion and artistic plot' was told that he would like to write such a work, but that he felt bound to continue to preach his message from the literary pulpit which had replaced the Arundel one.[25] Yet the concept of the artist as a communicator of God's truth was too deeply engrained in MacDonald for us ever to imagine him flouting it, and even when he wrote works in which the didacticism is not overt, such as the short novel called *The Portent*, he must have believed that they contained God's meaning. Even the fairytale, seemingly limited to the entertainment of child-minds, must have a meaning, he thought. 'It cannot help having some meaning; if it have proportion and harmony it has vitality, and vitality is truth. The beauty may be plainer in it than the truth, but without the truth the beauty could not be, and the fairytale would give no delight'.[26]

He expresses his sense of reality, and of the priorities arising from that sense, with particular clarity in another essay in *A Dish of Orts*. In 'A Sketch of Individual Development', he outlines what he conceives as being the natural series of stages of growth to God to which all humans tend. He imagines his human representative, at an advanced point of development, drawn towards the unseen.

> Life without the higher glory of the unspeakable, the atmosphere of a God, is not life, is not worth living. He would rather cease to be, than walk the dull level of the commonplace... Those who seem to him great, recognize the unseen — believe the roots of science to be therein hid — regard the bringing forth into sight of the things that are invisible as the end of all Art and every art — judge the true leader of men to be him who leads them closer to the essential facts of their being.[27]

So, not only did MacDonald tend to view the mundane world, which is what we are principally aware of, as insubstantial, transitory and dreamlike (as we have seen), but he also regarded it as lifeless and dull. Matter, as such, is dead, in the double sense that it lacks the life which is God and also lacks appeal to the human imagination — it is not interesting. Similarly, he rejected outlooks and philosophies which tended towards materialism. In MacDonald's eyes, true religion and genuine art pointed in the same direction — to God. An art which confined its response to the things of this world, however, was, he believed, an inferior art, as was an art which seemed to exist merely for its own sake. Poetry, he thought, was the highest art, and the poetic vision involved, for him, the revelation of the wonder and the meaning of existence. It is this bias in him which has made it seem to many readers that the novel, the form in which so much of his writing is cast, was the medium, with its commitment to the convincing rendering of the world of appearances, to which he was least suited.

Nevertheless, it is possible to exaggerate MacDonald's other-worldliness. He seldom forgets for long the limitations and difficulties of the actual human predicament. He rendered one of his favourite quotations from Novalis thus: 'Our life is *no dream*; but it ought to become one, and perhaps will' (my italics).[28] It is not so much that he regards the reality confronting man as dual; rather, it is man's vision which can be made to see in different ways. When Curdie cannot see Irene's grandmother in the attic, it shows the limitations of his vision, not the limitations of her reality. All that is needed is for him to improve, which he does later in the story. That which is divine in us has the capacity to see truly, but it is so often overlaid by our limited, material, mortal part. We inevitably fluctuate between the two, and so does

MacDonald's vision in his writing. The somewhat ironic account of MacDonald's tabletalk, given by Bernard Grenfell as part of his memories of the MacDonalds at Bordighera, serves as an amusing reminder of this oscillation: 'His method of passing without the least pause from a discussion on plum pudding to one on the immortality of the soul and then back again to plum pudding is rather startling to one unaccustomed to his books, where, I believe, he does the same thing'.[29] His writing is not an exhortation from someone already past the heavenly winning-tape: rather, it is a gasp of encouragement from a runner with several laps to go. Even as late as 1888, he was still writing with tentativeness: 'The universe would be to me no more than a pasteboard scene, all surface and no deepness, on the stage, if I did not hope in God. I will not say *believe*, for that is a big word, and it means so much more than my low beginnings of confidence'.[30]

Combined with this sense that he was sharing a predicament with his readers, however, is a somewhat contradictory air of leadership and challenge. He saw himself as one of those who 'recognize the unseen' and he attempted to be a true leader of men by bringing his readers 'closer to the essential facts of their being'. His books are an implicit but clear challenge — indeed, an affront — both in their unconventional natures and in the Christian message which can be found in them. In part, this is a matter of his famous rebellion against the prevailing harshness of the Calvinist theological tradition: his refusal to accept the notion of a God who could everlastingly damn most of his creatures appeals to us because it seems to locate him in a clear-cut and dramatic light. Nevertheless, this is only part of the religious concern of his books: his main religious challenge, to his own age and to ours, lies in his unrelenting opposition to the materialism of the modern outlook.

Nor is this spirit of opposition confined to unorthodoxy of form. Just as in his life he had a capacity for anger which could be awesome and powerful, so in his books his good characters consistently thwart, provoke and denounce evil in a spirit of conflict rather than conciliation and, furthermore, the reader is systematically provoked by the denial of what is expected or probable. MacDonald's desire to be seen to stand out against the prevailing view led him to exalt the stance of the outsider, in a way very much in line with Froude's assessment of the lack of freedom available for the open discussion of religious ideas in the 1860s: 'So far are we from free discussion that the world is not yet agreed that a free discussion is desirable; and till it be so agreed, the substantial intellect of the country will not throw itself into the question. *The battle will continue to be fought by outsiders, who suffice to disturb a repose which they cannot restore*' (my italics).[31] MacDonald was proud to be just such an outsider, both in the nonconformism which was his background, and in his overt stance of opposition to prevailing orthodoxies.

Much of MacDonald's writing has been rejected by twentieth-century readers on account of what is usually described as his tendency to preach, a characteristic which usually involves direct address to the reader and the manipulation of characters and events so as to engineer outcomes which clearly fit with his optimistic, Christian view of reality. His failure in these matters is normally ascribed either to incompetence or to a wilful (or financially enforced) refusal to stick to the unrealistic, fantasy forms which seem most in accord with his idealistic vision. It is in line with this view that his fairy and fantasy writing is held to be a success where the rest of his fiction seems to be a failure. While it is no part of my intention to deny the wonderful power and originality of MacDonald's achievement in the realm of fantasy, I wish also to make a case for the best of his other novels by exploring in detail the ways they are designed to work, and the rationale behind them. They are what they are, not (I believe) because of incompetence or because MacDonald did not really want to write them. Instead, they are to be seen as MacDonald's most ambitious, if flawed, attempts to articulate his vision in all its full meaning. This is particularly so of the novels set in Scotland, and it is on them, rather than on the English novels, that I concentrate in this study.

NOTES

1. Robert Lee Wolff, *The Golden Key: A Study of the Fiction of George MacDonald*, New Haven, 1961, p. 13.

2. Laurance J. Saunders, *Scottish Democracy 1815–1840: The Social and Intellectual Background*, Edinburgh & London, 1950, p. 197.

3. George Gray, *Recollections of Huntly as it was Seventy Years Ago*, Banff, 1892, p. 49.

4. David Fraser (ed.), *The Christian Watt Papers*, Edinburgh, 1983, pp. 28–29.

5. Gray, pp. 23, 11.

6. Gray, p. 67.

7. Greville MacDonald, *George MacDonald and his Wife*, second edition, London, 1924, p. 27. Henceforth, references to this basic source will be given in the text, using the abbreviation 'GMDW'.

8. Gray, p. 65n.

9. Robert Troup, *The Missionar Kirk of Huntly*, Huntly, Edinburgh & Glasgow, 1901, pp. 76–110.

10. Like most readers, I use the single-volume reprints of MacDonald's novels rather than the first editions. I therefore give page references to single-volume editions, but also provide chapter-numbers and titles (where available) in case of individual difficulties.

11. Letter of 5 November 1887, in Brander Library, Huntly.

12. Robert Sangster Rait, *The Universities of Aberdeen: A History*, Aberdeen, 1895, p. 220.

13. Alexander Findlay, *The Teaching of Chemistry in the Universities of Aberdeen* (Aberdeen University Studies no. 112), Aberdeen, 1935, pp. 49–57.

14. Robert E. Duncan, 'Artisans and proletarians: Chartism and working class allegiance in Aberdeen, 1838–1842', in *Northern Scotland* 4 (1–2), 1981, p. 63.

15. Wolff, pp. 16–17.

16. Richard H. Reis, *George MacDonald*, New York, 1972, p. 21. Also, George MacDonald, *Phantastes*, Everyman's Library, London, Melbourne & Toronto, 1983, p. v.

17. Harry Escott, *A History of Scottish Congregationalism*, Glasgow, 1960, p. 256.

18. David S. Robb, 'George MacDonald at Blackfriars Chapel' in *North Wind* 5 (1986), pp. 3–20.

19. Alexander Gammie, *The Churches of Aberdeen: Historical and Descriptive*, Aberdeen, 1909, p. 252.

20. George MacDonald, *Poetical Works*, 2 vols, London, 1893, I, p. 194.

21. William Gregory, *Letters to a Candid Inquirer on Animal Magnetism*, London, 1851. Also, *On the Theory of the Imagination, as explaining the Phenomena of Mesmerism; and on Money Challenges in Clairvoyance*, Edinburgh, 1852.

22. Letter in National Library of Scotland, MS.9745. 58.

23. Muriel Hutton, 'The George MacDonald Collection' in *Yale University Library Gazette* 51 (2), pp. 74–85 (pp. 77–78).

24. Ronald MacDonald, 'George MacDonald: A Personal Note' in *From a Northern Window*, ed. Frederick Watson, London, 1911, pp. 55–113 (pp. 66; 67–68).

25. Ronald MacDonald, p. 67.

26. George MacDonald, *A Dish of Orts*, London, 1893, p. 316.

27. *A Dish of Orts*, p. 58.

28. George MacDonald, *Phantastes* and *Lilith*, London, 1962, p. 180. All references to these works are to this edition.

29. Letter by Bernard Grenfell, quoted in correspondence in *English*, 11, no. 66 (Autumn, 1957), pp. 246–47.

30. Letter in National Library of Scotland, MS.9745. 68.

31. J. A. Froude, 'A Plea for the Free Discussion of Theological Difficulties' in *Essays in Literature and History*, London, n.d., pp. 195–223 (p. 223).

CHAPTER 2

NOVELS

It was part of the dreamlike unexpectedness of MacDonald's life that he found himself, in the early 1860s, turning to the writing of novels: when *David Elginbrod* was published in 1863, MacDonald was in his very late thirties — almost as old as a better-known late-starter was when he produced *Waverley*. As Greville records, the suggestion that MacDonald might work in the novel came from the publisher, George Murray Smith, who told him that 'if you would but write novels, you would find all the publishers saving up to buy them of you! Nothing but fiction pays' (GMDW p. 318). Smith was turning down MacDonald's play *If I had a Father*, which seems to have been written in 1859, so that whenever precisely the meeting was at which Smith offered his advice, it was some considerable time before MacDonald acted successfully upon it.

Greville MacDonald tells us of a failed attempt to turn *If I had a Father* into a novel, but apart from this, and the appearance of the short tale *The Portent* in 1860, there is a gap of five years between *Phantastes* (1858) and MacDonald's first published novel, a gap which even Greville finds 'curious' (GMDW, p. 318). It is worth bearing this delay in mind, as a qualification to the now standard view, put forward by C. S. Lewis in an aside in *The Allegory of Love*, that MacDonald, 'a mystic and natural symbolist', was driven by economic circumstances to the literary medium which made money.[1] Now it is true that novels provided his bread and butter, and that he regretted that he had to spend

27

so much time on them. What he wanted to do, of course, was to write poetry; he regarded the language of prose to be merely broken-down poetry (GMDW, p. 44). We may doubt, however, that we have been denied more works like *Phantastes* and *Lilith* just because MacDonald had to write what the public would pay for. All the evidence about MacDonald's personality suggests that had he felt strongly impelled to write another such work he would have found the opportunity to do so. Nor can his novels all be dismissed as grudging responses to financial pressure; the best of them, at least, seem to have been written not on necessity's terms, but on his own. Hence that considerable gap between Smith's advice and the appearance of *David Elginbrod* in 1863: MacDonald had to wait till he found the seed which suited him, and Greville tells how he discovered it in the famous Martin Elginbrodde epitaph (GMDW, p. 320). The other Scottish novels of the 1860s, *Alec Forbes of Howglen* and *Robert Falconer*, contain so much of himself — in the double sense of autobiography, and the sheer commitment which pervades them — that they cannot easily be dismissed as having been created against the grain, while MacDonald's elaborate and serious preparations for the writing of *Malcolm*, as sketched in by Greville (GMDW, pp. 418, 466), prepared the way for a massive two-work structure of great ambition. MacDonald may have been a whole lot of other things besides, but he was certainly a real novelist, in some sense of the word.

It has always been accepted that to write novels involves a commitment to portraying the mundane reality of everyday life. Nevertheless, the notion of the novel is a broad church and the Victorians, at least, sensibly retained some measure of distinction between different fictional effects by applying the term 'romance' to those works in which the author's imagination and

inventive powers made as obvious a contribution to the
end result as his powers of observation did. The word
also held out the promise of characters and incidents of
an exciting, striking, or melodramatic kind. Writers and
essayists debated vigorously the rival claims and merits
of the two approaches. When MacDonald began to
write novels in the 1860s, he was entering a scene in
which the possibilities seemed embodied in the realist
Trollope on the one hand, and in such romancers as
Dickens and Wilkie Collins on the other.

Nor, despite C. S. Lewis, was MacDonald's imagination
at home only in realms of mystical vision: he was very
engrossed in the problems of living in *this* world. In an
essay, full of good sense, by another product of King's
College, Aberdeen — Professor Herbert Grierson — we
find a consideration of this very question.

> Was George MacDonald a mystic? It was along
> the mystical line that he sought the solution of the
> enigma of sin and pain and death. But that is not
> sufficient to make one a mystic. For that one must
> have passed through the mystical experience. We
> know those who have so passed because they have
> no more doubts. They have seen and they believe,
> or rather know. They are no longer questers,
> doubting, inquiring, adumbrating allegorical
> arguers to the questions they are still really asking
> themselves. The great mystic proclaims...
> Compared with them George MacDonald is, like
> so many of his generation, a quester after a
> mystical solution rather than a mystic. What he
> utters is not so much a conviction he has attained
> to once and for all as a faith to which he
> passionately aspires — like Tennyson, or
> Browning, or F. D. Maurice. The nineteenth
> century was full of them.[2]

It is true, however, that MacDonald's goal in his

fiction was not confined to copying appearances. He
contemptuously rejected the merely material vision of
things as a vision of 'the commonplace'. Following his
beloved Novalis, it was his perennial desire to create a
romanticised vision of things — a process of 'investing
the commonplace with a lofty significance, the ordinary
with a mysterious aspect, the familiar with the prestige
of the unfamiliar, the finite with the semblance of
infinity'.[3] If the novel holds a mirror up to Nature,
MacDonald perceived that even mirrors transform as
they reflect. He makes the hero of a tale interpolated
into *Phantastes* muse on their power: 'What a strange
thing a mirror is! and what a wondrous affinity exists
between it and a man's imagination! For this room of
mine, as I behold it in the glass, is the same, and yet
not the same. It is not the mere representation of the
room I live in, but it looks just as if I were reading
about it in a story I like. All its commonness has
disappeared' (Ph, p. 94). It is as if he cannot conceive
of a story which does *not* have some measure of
transformational effect: literature, by its very nature,
seems at war with commonplaceness.

In his novels, more clearly and directly than in any
other literary medium, MacDonald was able to try to
achieve this Romantic transformation, and he used a
variety of means to make our commonplace world seem
strange and attractive, while familiar; however, it was
also urgent for MacDonald, the son of the Missionar
Kirk, as it was not for Novalis, to suggest that the
revealed strangeness and attractiveness within the
familiar was, ultimately, God himself. A swift survey of
the contents of each of the Scottish novels will indicate
that his debt to Romanticism was matched by an
equally strong debt to Christianity.

Each of his novels shows the emergence of the Christ-
principle. In several, the story that is told is of the
growth of the hero. In *David Elginbrod*, the growth is

purely moral: in a novel which moves from a Scottish landed estate to an English country house then on to London, the clever but incomplete youth who befriends David, the saintly estate foreman, and his family, but who neglects them after he moves to a new post as tutor and has his first experiences with love and evil, eventually comes to understand the reality of God — and his own failings — and returns to marry Margaret, the Elginbrods' daughter. In *Robert Falconer* (1868), on the other hand, the hero of the title has comparatively little moral growth to achieve, but he journeys through a longer tract of life than perhaps any other MacDonald hero in his instinctive search for the way to fully release the Christ within himself. The puritanically rigid outlook of his grandmother and her self-torturing belief in a God of wrath and damnation (the Huntly-based opening portion of the book, telling of Robert's boyhood in the care of this orthodoxly Calvinist but loving old lady, is its most memorable part) constitute the first of several bleak phases of life which Robert has to encounter, suffer from, and transcend as he matures through disappointments in love and friendship, and finally descends into the hell of the London slums in the search for his long-lost father. It is while engaged in this search that he is transformed into a Christ-like social worker. In *Alec Forbes of Howglen* (1865), which is confined to scenes based on Huntly and Aberdeen, both physical and moral growth are involved: Alec's zestful rural boyhood gives way to the painful experience and self-knowledge of undergraduate adolescence. His recovery from sorrow and from the degradation of drink and loose women paves the way to a maturity which confirms his original Christ-like promise. The motif of being confronted by a seemingly endless bleakness — the essence of the story to be told in *Robert Falconer* — is here focused on the heroine, the orphan Annie Anderson. These novels all contain important elements of autobiography.

In many of the later novels, the triumph of the Christ-principle is not so much a matter of growth internal to a character, but involves, rather, the eventual establishment in a position of social authority (usually, an aristocratic rank involving control of an estate) of a hero who has a right (either a moral right, or a hitherto unrealised hereditary one) to it. The Portlossie novels (*Malcolm*, 1875, and *The Marquis of Lossie*, 1877) and *Sir Gibbie* (1879) are the clearest and finest examples from this phase. All these later novels are less autobiographical than their predecessors, something which is superficially indicated by their use of settings other than Huntly and Aberdeen: Portlossie is sited on the Banffshire coast, while much of *Sir Gibbie* takes place in the valley of the Dee. Of the still later novels, most are set in an unspecified rural Scotland, though *What's Mine's Mine* (1886), a work dealing with contemporary social and economic developments in the Highlands, is located, vaguely, on the west coast. In the later works, the triumph of Christ is given a variety of forms. In *Castle Warlock* (1882), a threatened loss of ownership of the hereditary family possession is averted by the discovery of treasure hidden within the walls. *Donal Grant* (1883) tells of the arrival of the peasant-hero as tutor within an aristocratic household: through his efforts, the castle is cleansed of its murky secrets, the heiress saved from a fate worse than, but including, death, and Donal eventually left as master of the estate. In *What's Mine's Mine*, worldliness is represented by a *nouveau riche* English distiller who buys a Highland estate and clears off the remnants of the local clan. This last is led by a young chief and his brother, who are unable to prevent the clearance, but who lead their people to a new life in Canada. The Christian message of this novel is that despite the triumph of materialism here, the faithful have an alternative domain to which they can repair under the leadership of their righteous master.

The last three Scottish novels are all much briefer than
the foregoing: *The Elect Lady* (1888), *Heather and Snow*
(1893), and *Salted With Fire* (1897). The weakest of all
MacDonald's Scottish novels, *The Elect Lady*, tells of the
loss and rediscovery of a Grail-like chalice made by
Benvenuto Cellini, while the last two are tales of the
painful disciplining of sinning young men whose transgressions are viewed with vastly more condemnation
than those of Alec Forbes twenty-five years earlier. A
darkening of outlook in his later years is one of the
developments a discussion of MacDonald must record.

MacDonald hints at the estranging presence of the
divine within commonplace reality by means of a wide
variety of techniques which all tend in the direction of
retreating from mimetic illusion. For one thing, he was
not afraid to use the perennial clichés and archetypes of
popular fiction and drama; indeed, he seems to have
positively welcomed them, seeing them as harmonising
with our deepest hopes and fears. Wilfred Cumbermede,
one of several of his heroes who follow their creator
into novel-writing, says of some of his earliest tale-
telling experiences as a boy: 'My favourite invention...
was of a youth in humble life who found at length he
was of far other origin than he had supposed. I did not
know then that the fancy, not uncommon with boys,
has its roots in the deepest instincts of our human
nature' (WC, p. 75). Thus, the stereotyped charac-
terisation, which commentators on MacDonald have
complained of in the past, may well have been a
matter of choice rather than incompetence or haste.[4]
Much of the action in these novels is the common stuff
of daydreams: heroines are rescued from floods and
blizzards; aristocratic rivals are outfaced and defeated
in love; evil people and evil attitudes are trounced, in
argument and sometimes physically; the hero is an
unfailing help and support to the poor, weak and
oppressed; after seemingly endless trials and setbacks,
the righteous are given dominion of their world.

In a sense, these daydreams are unreal: the world of experience is not always like that. In another sense, they are thoroughly real, in that such dreams, desires and impulses are part of the inner experience of us all. Making his external fictional reality out of internal psychological reality was one of the most important ways he adopted of endowing 'the ordinary with a mysterious aspect'; another was to set most of his best fiction in a region which partook both of ordinariness and mystery — the Scotland of his youth.

In these novels, much which seems the product of a fertile Romantic imagination can be traced back to the world of MacDonald's boyhood, as many details testify. To the Victorian reader, Scotland was still a country known through books, reputation and myth rather than through direct knowledge, and was already being thought of as the domain of untold eccentricities. Colourful behaviour could be located there without straining the reader's sense of credibility. In her *Autobiography*, MacDonald's friend Margaret Oliphant recalls how, in *Salem Chapel* (1863), she based her picture of English Dissenting manners on some exiled Scots who attended the Free Church of Scotland in Liverpool. As she phrases it, it is clear that the delightful eccentricities she portrays in that novel would not have been regarded as quite so extraordinary if she had retained the Scottish reference: '*The saving grace of their Scotchness being withdrawn* [my italics], they became still more wonderful as Dissenting deacons, and the truth of the picture was applauded to all the echoes'.[5]

Scotland, therefore, could function, for novelists of the 1860s, as a region where wonder and strangeness were domesticated: MacDonald had only to delineate the world of his boyhood, in word and deed, to be able to offer his readers a transformed reality. Realism, when applied to Scotland, produced a world of Romance: it was the same formula Scott had stumbled upon.

The virtues of MacDonald's renderings of Scottish town and country life have long been acknowledged. Place and setting are important in the best of his work: the natural world is a pressing presence, as it is in Emily Bronte or Hardy. Even readers unfamiliar with Aberdeenshire can sense how precisely MacDonald locates his characters in landscapes and townscapes which are part remembered, part imagined in accordance with the needs of each book. The 'Rothieden' of *Robert Falconer*, as befits a tale of escape from bleakness and joylessness, offers a Huntly which is principally a place of interiors, and in which the outer world, when we are aware of it, is frequently a region of darkness and cold. ('Rothie' is a regional word meaning 'tumult', 'uproar' or 'muddle' while a 'den' is a narrow, wooded valley; more often than not, MacDonald's innocent-seeming Scots names carry their own load of meaning.) *Alec Forbes*, on the other hand, portrays Huntly as 'Glamerton', and much of its glamour consists in its interfusion with the surrounding countryside of field and river, and its openness to the seasons and rhythms of nature. The extraordinary sense of characters and action being located in an environment at once solidly real and glowingly attractive (despite the destructive capacity nature reveals) is a major source of the strength of this novel, and the same can be said, perhaps even more forcefully, of *Malcolm*. In this later novel, MacDonald is using a setting which the mind can grasp almost as a single totality: Cullen Bay's long curve of sand, its small two-tier town at one end and the cliffs containing the Preaching Cave at the other, and, behind everything, the extensive policies of Cullen House, constitutes a vast stage-set containing all the elements which MacDonald needs to tell his tale of man's social and eternal existences. Place is important in *Malcolm* above all: it tells the tale of the discovery of an alternative, hidden geography within the landscape — a geography of

crucial importance to the hero's knowledge of himself.
The sense of place is not merely one of the delights of
MacDonald's best fiction — it is part of its meaning,
just as it is, in no very different way, in his fantasy
works.

At his best, MacDonald offers much which relates
him to the Scottish tradition of social realism in fiction,
even though that factual solidity is designed to offer the
reader an unfamiliar, not an everyday, sense of reality.
In this, his ability to reproduce Scots speech is one of
his major strengths, however much of a drawback it
may be to readers unfamiliar with Scots and, especially,
with the speech of the North-east. For he makes the
bold — indeed, the defiant — decision to challenge his
readers with a strongly regional Scots vernacular lying
somewhere between standard literary Scots and the
daunting language of, say, *Johnnie Gibb of Gushetneuk*.
The gauntlet is thrown down in the opening words of
David Elginbrod (words which are juxtaposed with a
chapter-motto of substantially modernised Chaucer):
'Meg! whaur are ye gaein' that get, like a wull shuttle?
Come in to the beuk'. With this magnificent gesture,
MacDonald embarked on a novel-writing career which
made him, among other claims to distinction, one of
the leading writers of Scots prose in the nineteenth
century. There is less Scots in this first novel, taken as a
whole, than there would be in later ones, and some of it
is offered with the air of the set-piece. Yet David's
prayers have a true rhetorical grandeur, and the more
conversational passages of Scots are capable of moments
of delightful vigour: 'I dinna care the black afore my
nails for ony skelp-doup o' the lot o' ye' (DE, p. 49; I,
10, 'Harvest'). Such a sentence does more to conjure up
a full social reality than many a paragraph of
description. In the later novels of the 1860s and 1870s,
the sheer quantity of Scots increases substantially, until,
in *Malcolm*, one feels that the language is being used,

not with any literary self-consciousness or with any
rhetorical goal in view, but merely because MacDonald
is imagining his characters speaking that way.
Occasionally, Scots is used to comic effect but with
none of the air of patronage that can mar vernacular
comedy in later writers, and the emotional range to
which he applies Scots is markedly wide. An example
will illustrate MacDonald's ear for the strong
downrightness of Scots. David Elginbrod is refusing to
acquiesce in the laird's demand that he discourage
Hugh Sutherland from visiting him and his family:

> 'Na, na; as lang's I hae a door to haud open, it's
> no to be steekit to him.'
> 'Efter a', the door's mine, Dawvid,' said the laird.
> 'As lang's I'm in your hoose an' in your service,
> sir, the door's mine,' retorted David, quietly. (DE,
> p. 28; I, 6, 'The Laird's Lady')

For both the quantity and quality of his Scots prose,
MacDonald deserves a secure place in our picture of
Scottish fiction. Its excellence is not merely the result of
his knowing the words and pronunciations but arises, as
is true of all such linguistic mastery, because his mind
and personality are inward with the characteristic
outlook of the society which used them. The ability to
reproduce so faithfully the speech of this far-flung
region derives from the same Scottish country roots as,
for example, his not-so-Victorian freedom in writing
about exposed female legs, or the use of prostitutes, or
in his occasional earthiness of language. His evident,
and explicit, love for the Scots tongue is a facet of his
feelings for the country which formed him.

The Scots vernacular in these novels goes a long way
to implying the presence of a whole community and
way of life. In other respects, however, it is broadly
true, as Colin Manlove has said, that 'he has perhaps
not so much grasp of his villages as whole communities

as of individuals who stand out even while they
belong'.[6] MacDonald's concentration on places and on
memorable individuals arises because his main
protagonists are children or young people: his novels
therefore tend to reflect the priorities in the
consciousnesses of the young, whose worlds are made
up of what is immediately visible and important to
them but who lack the overview of the historian — or
of the all-seeing narrator of *Sunset Song*. The selection of
this youthful angle on the world is one of the most
important means by which he attains his aim of
bringing out the wonder of the everyday. This is most
apparent of all in those portions of such books as *Alec
Forbes* and *Robert Falconer* which deal with the early
years of their central figures. There, childhood worlds
are evoked with such fidelity and vitality that
MacDonald, for the moment, approaches comparison
with the Dickens of *David Copperfield* and the George
Eliot of *The Mill on the Floss*. And even when heroes
and heroines have grown up, the sensibility through
which the tales are mediated is still, subtly, that of
youth so that the world evoked in the fiction retains its
fresh glamour and the moments of tension and
melodrama distill their full intensity. Not only are we
more than recompensed, by the vividness of the
'Huntly' experiences of Alec Forbes, Annie Anderson
and Robert Falconer, for the absence of the full social
dimension which we have come to expect from Scottish
rural fiction, but the intimate point of view of
MacDonald's novels avoids that critically distanced
attitude to the country town which was to become a
cliché of later Scottish fiction. Despite their failings,
Glamerton and Rothieden are not issues in themselves,
as Barbie, Kinraddie and Segget are.

   That it is not one of MacDonald's priorities to focus
on his villages as whole communities is further signalled
by another aspect of his novels. In Scottish fiction

where the community as a whole *is* an important element in meaning and design, narrators tend to be chosen who are themselves part of the community, whether they are fully achieved characters like the dominie in *A Window in Thrums*, or felt presences like the narrator of *The House With The Green Shutters*, or the community voices which alternate with Chris as the main consciousness in *A Scots Quair*. Although MacDonald's underlying point of view is that of the youthful characters at the centre of his stories, the overt viewpoint is that of a narrator who seems hardly to be distinguished from the author himself — so much so that, despite the theoretical problems, it is most convenient to refer to the narrator simply as 'MacDonald'. (The attempt in *Robert Falconer* to introduce one of Falconer's London disciples as narrator is so perfunctory that it can almost be ignored.) This in turn leads us to touch on that oft-repeated complaint about the novels, their 'preaching'.

MacDonald's presence in his own works is not achieved merely through passages of direct address to the reader: such passages, in fact, are not so frequent in the earlier novels, although they are found there occasionally and become much more prominent from *Sir Gibbie* onwards. When such passages do occur, however, they obtrude less than might have been expected, because even the standard narrative is written in a style steeped in personality. The speaking-voice which MacDonald chooses for his narration modulates easily and frequently into a style compounded of the poetic and the rhetorical: it is a forceful and (once adjusted to) surprisingly readable combination. Nor are the embedded 'sermons' the only set-piece passages of authorial intrusion. Some of his descriptions of nature are so poetically imbued with animistic imagery that we are vividly aware of the man writing the words. The excellence of his Scots prose can make his English seem ponderous and calculated at times, but, despite occasional lapses, he usually writes with the poise, force and effortless vitality of a confident Victorian stylist; despite its frequent lushness, his English is as firmly founded on the speaking voice as his Scots. When to such signs of a particular personality we add the weight of the other distinctive attributes of these works (their idealistic tone, their characteristic values and concerns, their powerful regionalism, their overt optimism, etc) we are driven to the conclusion that a large part of whatever appeal they may have is the appeal of contact with MacDonald himself. Although modern taste in fiction does not readily approve of novels being used as vehicles for the overt and unironic presentation of an author's views and personality, MacDonald was writing in an age with no such scruples.

The projection of an author's personality is not merely a matter of self-indulgence: it was a technique widely used, especially by those prose-writers often now called the Victorian Sages, to make an argument more persuasive.[7] The Victorian reader desired not merely to believe in a point of view; he preferred to believe in a person, and would do so if he sensed the point of view being urged by an attractive, sympathetic, powerful or trustworthy personality. By various means, MacDonald does create such an image of himself for the readers of his novels: he had as an example not merely such contemporaries as Carlyle or Ruskin but also the supreme example of Christ, for (like many others) he thought of the New Testament as containing not merely Christ's story and values but also the possibility of a living contact with the man himself.

An unexpected result of MacDonald's palpable presence, almost as a character, in his own novels is the adjustment it entails in the relationship between himself and his characters. Rubbing shoulders with the creatures of his imagination, he is in a less authoritative position, as it were, than most novelists are in dictating and defining our knowledge of their characters. MacDonald's are given a kind of equality of status with him, and (by extension) with us. The fictional world they inhabit seems, as we read, less of a thing apart from us: MacDonald himself blurs that seemingly inevitable distinction, and our imaginative participation in their lives is thereby heightened. We are moved more by what they are and do, rather than by what we are told to think about them, though the latter might have been expected in tales with such a manifest intention for us. Indeed, there are numerous occasions when MacDonald the narrator expresses ignorance as to what a character is feeling or believing: they have, for him, their own reality which is, ultimately, a facet of God's mysterious Creation, and MacDonald is content at times not to pry beyond their visible behaviour. Hence, perhaps, the characteristically strong openings that he gives his books: he is a master of the arresting action, scene, speech or description with which to seize our attention at the outset. It is his residual Calvinism which lies at the heart of this authorial modesty: God, not man, is the author of all things, he believed, and in his essay on 'The Imagination: Its Functions and its Culture' he denies any ultimate creativeness to man. Despite Coleridge, MacDonald the Missionar ascribes *all* creativity to the Creator; man's function is much more lowly — even the artist's. 'Is not the *Poet*, the *Maker*, a less suitable name for him than the *Trouvere*, the *Finder*?'[8] The deep-seated sense of child-like, wide-eyed discovery is among the chief sources of the dream-like wonder with which MacDonald's rendering of the everyday is tinged in these works: once again, as we read, we become, with the characters and with MacDonald himself, children or young people embarking on the journey of life. His fiction forces us to become as little children, in the hope that it might thereby help us to enter into the kingdom of heaven.

Despite the welter of experiences which make up a MacDonald novel — a welter which parallels life itself — it usually has a powerful underlying sense of direction and of structure: the underlying goal of life has its counterpart in an assured fictional resolution. At first glance, these long novels seem examples of the worst kind of shapeless, self-indulgent Victorian fictional excess. No brief discussion here can finally dispel that impression; only a sympathetic reading can do that. Nevertheless, it is possible to suggest some of MacDonald's structural power by considering *Alec Forbes of Howglen*, a novel which is arguably his best and which illustrates many of the general points of this chapter.

This work is unusual in his output in that it focuses on not one character but two. Alongside the tale of Alec's growth from pre-adolescent blessedness, through the pains and disappointments of first love, to a mature wisdom which involves self-command, coming to God and the realisation that the heroine, Annie Anderson, is the girl he ought to marry, we find the story of Annie herself. The novel begins with the funeral of her father, whose death leaves her a nine-year old orphan, without a home of her own, despite the modest legacy she has been left. After a few months of being cared for on her father's farm by her aunt, she is passed to the care of a grasping shopkeeper in nearby Glamerton, Robert Bruce, a cousin whose household is now technically her home but which fails to provide any of the loving care which gives that word meaning. (Bruce is deliberately named after Scotland's great hero-king in order to embody a strain of satiric criticism of the pretensions of nineteenth-century Scotland. A heroic past had given way, it seemed, to a small-minded, mercantile present.)

Annie's troubles are compounded when she is sent to school and encounters the brutal regime of 'Murder' Malison, but the school's ethos of punishment is mitigated for Annie by the presence of Alec, a little older than herself and a natural leader who takes her under his wing. Their schooldays together are thus a compound of bleakness and glory, with the blight of Malison and the Bruces failing to neutralise the idyll of childhood vitality freely at large in the domain of nature. Annie has a further trial to bear, as her powerful instinct to seek God leads her to encounter the terrors of Calvinist doctrine. She finds protection from the human mind's misconception (as MacDonald views it) of a god of wrathful punishment, in the human heart's kindness which she prompts in most of those around her, and she grows into a loving and beloved member of the community, her natural holiness flowering in a most natural and convincing way. Alec, on the other hand, goes to the nearby university where he makes a mortal enemy of a villainous young aristocrat, Patrick Beauchamp. He also falls in love with the neurotic Kate Fraser, but losing her to Beauchamp plunges him into a fit of alcoholic dissipation. He recovers with the help of his eccentric friend Cosmo Cupples, a drunken librarian whose life has been blighted by a similar disappointment in love. Annie becomes more and more involved in the affairs of her friends the Forbes, who are financially at the mercy of Robert Bruce and who are saved, without their knowledge, by Annie's sacrifice of her own modest fortune. The stories of the two young people remain gently intertwined throughout this long and leisurely novel: they dance their sober dance through youth until the inevitable, but satisfying, marriage-ending.

Strong as it is, this double narrative does not carry alone the structural weight of the novel: for one thing, it is reinforced by an awareness of the shaping structures within the world it depicts. The life of the countryside colours all with the passage of the seasons: the young people register the phases of the year directly when they play as children, and when they reach their teens MacDonald echoes the rhythms of the Scottish Victorian student's year (five winter months at university, seven at home or earning money) by having Annie act as companion to Alec's mother, only to be banished back to the Bruces when Alec returns home. (The snobbish Mrs. Forbes fears emotional developments between Annie and her son.) Furthermore, the growth of the two, from childhood to early adulthood, is firmly but sensitively done, so that, once again, the reader feels in contact with the slow, deep rhythms within human experience. We are aware, too, as we read, that the novel is controlled by MacDonald's thematic concerns. Not only does Alec's story articulate the archetypal pattern of the happy fall from innocence into sinning experience which is followed by a more morally elevated perfection, but the theme of Annie's homeless-ness — moving enough when it is applied to the young child — gains in power when it persists in the life of the young woman, until a final expulsion from Howglen when the shipwrecked Alec is brought home and Annie slips out into night-time Glamerton, as homeless as she has ever been. At a moment like this, the sheer previous bulk of the novel tells.

MacDonald's delineation of human growth is not only central to his theme of how we come to God but it is immensely satisfying in itself, helping endow the work with that pervasive air of youthfulness and freshness which is one of its main appeals. The youthful viewpoint which produces this general effect is capable, too, of controlling individual scenes and strands, endowing them with a notable subjective intensity. To take one example, the villainous Beauchamp is, by the standards of conventional realism, an unlikely, demonic creature.

His vindictive malevolence against Alec leads him so
far in his spite as to seduce the affections of Kate
Fraser, dominating her by the cynical manipulation
of her hypersensitivity. Indeed, in his persistent
following of Alec in the search for a way to harm him,
he comes to seem an almost supernatural creature,
haunting his prey with the tenacity of Frankenstein's
monster. It is eventually no surprise that he finally
attempts to murder Alec directly.

How did such a being find his way into this novel of
quiet optimism and partial autobiography? He gets in
during a scene in which Alec, having turned to
medicine, is imagined arriving for his first lesson in
dissection. Understandably keyed up, he enters the
lecture room acutely aware both of the demonstrator's
table ('not daring to glance at something which lay
upon it') and of the hearty bravado of the other
students to whom his obvious squeamishness is a source
of mirth. When he does look at the corpse, his sense of
the outrageousness of the situation is heightened as he
discovers it to be that of a beautiful young woman. The
body occasions a 'brutal jest' from one of the students,
Beauchamp, who then insults the sensitive newcomer.
Not only is this convincing scene envisaged, in general
terms, from Alec's standpoint, but MacDonald goes one
step further in making Alec's precise feelings and
interpretations the book's truth: he writes as if what
Alec *seemed* to perceive was actually taking place, as
when he looks at the corpse with the 'brutal jest'
ringing in his ears:

> In vain the upturned face made its white appeal to
> the universe; a laugh billowed the silence about its
> head.
>
> But no rudeness could hurt that motionless heart
> — no insult bring a blush on that pale face. The
> closed eyes, the abandoned hands seemed only to
> pray:

'Let me into the dark — out of the eyes of those men!' (AF, p. 155; Chap. 36)

Beauchamp, in fact, is introduced into the novel in a scene in which the subjective feelings of the hero are given the status of autonomous fictional facts, and this pattern is maintained throughout, at least as far as Beauchamp is concerned. It is not just that one lovelorn young man, cut out by another, feels as if his rival must have some devilish power and intent: MacDonald goes some considerable way in actually granting Beauchamp that power and intent. Similarly, when Kate fails to respond to Alec's ardour (even before Beauchamp cuts in), we are given to understand that not merely does Alec feel hurt and frustrated by her behaviour but also that there is something temperamentally wrong with her very nature: once again, the subjective perception of the hero is made the novel's objective fact.

Melodrama, therefore, finds its way into the novel, to create a pattern whereby the underlying rhythm of quiet growth is overlaid by a layer of eventfulness and tension. The world of MacDonald's childhood provided, in actuality, many sources of melodramatic excitement: the flood which sweeps away one of the town's bridges and provides the occasion for Alec's heroic rescue of Annie from the flooded cottage (the events of 1829 still alive in MacDonald's memory), the brutality of an unreformed schoolhouse, the psychological terrors of Calvinist dogma and the heightened superstitiousness of a phase of local religious revivalism, the drama of a Missionar expulsion (though MacDonald, by making the accused Robert Bruce actually present, gives this scene a forensic edge which few such moments could actually have had). Even Alec's escape from an Aberdeen mob which suspects him (because he is a medical student) of grave-robbing is derived from events in that city in 1831, and his final experiences in the Arctic, as surgeon on board a whaler, are a reminder of the importance of that industry in the major east-coast ports during the nineteenth century. Add to this the juvenile intensities of gang activities and vendettas, and youthful disasters like the boating accident which overtakes Alec's home-made craft, and one can see that the world of *Alec Forbes* is a world full of melodramatic potential. When this world is viewed with the subjective intensity of MacDonald's treatment, the effect is of a glowing heightening of reality.

It is not merely certain situations which MacDonald endows with special imaginative life: characters, too, have the same memorable largeness. MacDonald was writing in an age which, unlike the present one, regarded the encounter with fictional character as one of the reasons for reading a novel; the practice is justified here (if it needs justification) in that the encounter with a series of characters is, in a sense, the story that is being told of the hero and heroine. 'Experience', which conditions the growth of the central figures, consists largely of the personalities, behaviour and ideas of the people they meet. Annie, therefore, is first of all entrapped in the loveless selfishness of Bruce and his household, and finds her life being made even more bleak by Malison's schoolroom regime and by the hell-fire beliefs of those she meets in the Missionar Kirk. These blights are mitigated for her by her dealings with Alec and his mother, and with what is loving and humane in Missionars such as Thomas Crann the stonemason, and blind Tibbie Dyster. Alec's boyhood supremacy is shown in his triumphant opposition to such incarnations of wrong as Robert Bruce (and his dog) and the unreformed Malison. When he goes to university, his difficulties are incarnated in Kate Fraser and Patrick Beauchamp; the power which pulls him through is embodied in the delightfully original Cupples. In MacDonald's dreamlike experience, the directions dictated by such personalities as his father,

John Kennedy, William Gregory, A. J. Scott, and several others encouraged him to think of life less as a domain of inner moral conflict and self-formation (as George Eliot does, for example) than as a journey, the direction and success of which is considerably dictated by the fellow-travellers whom one meets.

MacDonald, therefore, needed characters with their own self-contained vitality. How does he achieve this? In the best cases — Thomas Crann, Tibbie, Cupples — their Scots speech has much to do with it. From the time of Scott — and of the *Noctes Ambrosianae* — onwards, writers had been aware that vernacular Scots has a tendency, in fiction, to give the character that uses it a particular detached prominence, a slightly artificial vividness. In an ironic or comic context the result can veer towards the patronising, but handled respectfully good Scots dialogue can provide a matchless concentration of imaginative weight and force, as many Scottish novelists of the nineteenth and twentieth centuries have demonstrated. MacDonald, at his best (as here), is of their company. As it happens, there is also a good deal of humour in MacDonald's finest novels, and Scots often gives it an extra edge; it arises spontaneously in the writing, however, without that air of calculation in which Barrie's humourous portraits are steeped.

The prominent characters surrounding Alec and Annie are further helped to attain the requisite imaginative independence through their dream-like unexpectedness. Just as Beauchamp is unpredictable in being a villainous, aristocratic medical student, so the others enter the novel with an air of being discovered which immediately marks them out as the originals they are. Thomas Crann and Robert Bruce instantly tell in the masterly, concentrated opening chapter; Tibbie immediately holds the attention of both Annie and the reader when she is glimpsed, in church, her

obviously blind eyes directed upward to the sunlight
which travels round the interior; so (above all) Cupples
grips us when Alec visits his hitherto unsuspected attic
to find the brusque, scruffy, knowledgeable, lively-
minded, cynical and alcoholic librarian who can dismiss
him again with 'Weel, cut yer stick. I hae eneuch o' ye
for ae nicht. I canna stan' glowerin' een, especially i'
the heids o' idiots o' innocents like you' (AF, p. 172;
Chap. 39).

The factor which finally seals the weight and vital
interest of such characters is the way in which they are
made to combine authority and fallibility. It is not just
that they are realistically flawed, their two-sided moral
status making them a recognisable human mixture. The
two aspects of their moral dimension, in fact, do not
coalesce into a comfortable greyness; rather, they war
within each character, giving them an inner fire and
making of each a paradox. The function of these
characters is to aid and direct the hero and heroine on
the road to God: their authority enables them to do
this, but their failings enable their young charges to
surpass them. When, in turn, Alec and Annie act as
guides and examples to them, it is a sign that their
divine goals have been reached.

The reaching of a goal is a common conclusion for a
narrative, but the difficulties and dangers in this story
are so many and so intransigent that their overcoming
has a quality of the wonderful; the transition from
desperate travail to secure felicity is so complete that it
has some of the quality of the fairytale. Indeed, as I have
discussed elsewhere, this novel, like all MacDonald's
'realistic' novels, has many fairytale characteristics,
both overt and subtle.[9] It has its openly fairytale
counterpart in the short story, 'The Golden Key',
written at about the same time and published two
years later in 1867. This, too, has the double emphasis
on a hero and heroine who journey together through

life, become separated for a time, but reunite to share in the most miraculous part of the journey. In the novel, the heroine, despite her potent and unfailing goodness, serves the principal plot function of needing frequent rescue, from rats, from bullying, from terror, from floods, from hypothermia, from homelessness and, Cinderella-like, from being undervalued in the humble circumstances which obscure her inner worth; the hero, despite his flaws, is essentially a rescuer, of Annie and others. Like Mossy and Tangle in 'The Golden Key', Alec and Annie age only outwardly; within themselves, where we the readers know them, they remain the young children we first encounter, just as the heroes and heroines of fairy-tales never grow old and, being completely identified with in their dynamic youthfulness, impart that youthfulness to their readers of whatever age. The rich wonder of the world of the fairytale colours even this novel, prosaically accurate in its depiction of nineteenth-century Scotland in so many ways. The combination results in a minor masterpiece which only George MacDonald could have written.

NOTES

1. C. S. Lewis, *The Allegory of Love: A Study in Medieval Tradition*, London & Oxford, 1936, p. 232.
2. H. J. C. Grierson, 'George MacDonald' in *The Aberdeen University Review* XII, 34, November 1924, pp. 1–13 (p. 11).
3. Novalis, *Fragmente des Jahres 1798, Gesammelte Werke*, No. 879, vol. III, p. 38, reprinted in *European Romanticism: Self-Definition*, edited by Lilian R. Furst, London & New York, 1980, p. 3.
4. Richard H. Reis, *George MacDonald*, New York, 1972, p. 67.
5. Mrs. Harry Coghill (ed.), *Autobiography and Letters of Mrs. Margaret Oliphant*, Leicester, 1974, p. 84.
6. Colin Manlove, 'George MacDonald's Early Scottish Novels' in *Nineteenth-Century Scottish Fiction: Critical Essays* edited by Ian Campbell, Manchester, 1979, pp. 68–88 (p. 72).
7. John Holloway, *The Victorian Sage: Studies in Argument*, London, 1953, pp. 164–65.

8. George MacDonald, *A Dish of Orts*, London, 1893, p. 20.

9. See my essay, 'George MacDonald's Aberdeenshire Fairytale' in *Studies in Scottish Fiction: Nineteenth Century*, eds Horst W. Drescher and Joachim Schwend, Frankfurt am Main, Bern, New York, 1985, pp. 205–16.

CHAPTER 3

SYMBOLISM AND ALLEGORY

'Is not the *Poet*, the *Maker*, a less suitable name for him than the *Trouvere*, the *Finder*?', asks MacDonald. Strangely, to our minds, he denies to the poet any ultimate originality: the poet cannot create, but can only discover that which has already been created. And what was it that MacDonald's poet was to find? 'The bringing forth into sight of the things that are invisible [is] the end of all Art and every art'. Hidden meanings are all around us: 'The forms of Nature are the representations of human thought in virtue of their being the embodiment of God's thought... The man, then, who, in harmony with nature, attempts the discovery of more of her meanings, is just searching out the things of God.' As MacDonald had said slightly earlier in the essay from which this last quotation is taken, 'The meanings are in those forms already'. In creating the world, God had apparently devised a vast reservoir of divine utterances.[1]

The notion that there is a dimension of reality behind, and greater than, the appearances revealed by the senses was frequently to be found, of course, in Romantic thought, but MacDonald applied it with such minute precision and specific Christian reference that he seems to have as much kinship with Dante (whose work he knew and revered) as he has with Novalis or Wordsworth. The medieval concept of the world as God's book made a lot of sense to MacDonald — he uses the idea himself on occasion, as when he asks, 'Shall God's fiction, which is man's reality, fall short of man's fiction?'[2] It was an image which satisfied his sense of the vital meaningfulness of even the smallest particle of human experience and observation, as well as his belief in the universal harmony. Furthermore, the idea of God as author suggested the nearness and intimacy which MacDonald sought for in his understanding of God, as when Margaret Elginbrod's instinctive love of nature is ascribed to her 'desire to read the word of God in his own handwriting' (DE, p. 40; I, 9, 'Nature').

His belief that the world is a book, given pattern and significance by a writer-god, is an echo of pre-scientific medieval ways of thought. Modern man, however, needs both the modern and ancient ways of seeing and understanding, a duality the hero of one of his later novels, Cosmo Warlock, sustains: 'There was in him an unusual combination of the power to read the hieroglyphic aspect of things, and the scientific nature that bows before fact' (CW, p. 5; Chap. 1, 'Castle Warlock'). Therefore, although the poet loses, in MacDonald's scheme, the dignity of originating his own mental inventions, he gains the compensating dignity of the seer, the visionary with the power of reading 'the hieroglyphic aspect of things'.

The power which grants this visionary ability is the imagination, and MacDonald is even more extreme and explicit than Coleridge in underlining the divine source of this faculty. Where, for Coleridge, the primary imagination was 'a repetition in the finite mind of the eternal act of creation in the infinite I AM', and the secondary imagination a power seeking unity and striving to enliven that which is dead, MacDonald displaces the notion of mere resemblance to God with that of identity with God: he calls a wise imagination 'the presence of the spirit of God'.[3] Coleridge's notion of the imagination as the faculty of perception is profound enough, but MacDonald goes even further in identifying it with that which is divine in us — with what he calls, in one of his major poetic efforts, *The Diary of an Old Soul*, the 'Christ-self'.[4] Coming to God — reuniting with our creator — therefore, is not to be envisaged only as letting the Christ-principle emerge to guide our lives and beliefs; it is a matter of liberating and valuing our imaginations. Believing that man in his very nature leans towards reuniting with God, so he also believed that man is, in his deepest being, a poet and that artistic utterance is a natural and important function. Hence the many poets, novelists and musicians among his heroes; he signals goodness in his characters by their responsiveness to art.

The poet's task, therefore, is to discover the meanings that are in nature's forms already, and to communicate the joyful news about them in art. (North Wind tells little Diamond that 'A poet is a man who is glad of something, and tries to make other people glad of it too'.)[5] Nature, however, also provides the only available means of communicating ideas between men. MacDonald imagines a man with a thought in his mind and the desire to communicate it, but who is thwarted because, within himself, he has no means of sharing his idea with another. 'Gazing about him in pain, he suddenly beholds the material form of his immaterial condition. There stands his thought! God thought it before him, and put its picture there ready for him when he wanted it... This he seizes as the symbol, as the garment or body of his invisible thought, presents it to his friend, and his friend understands him'.[6] MacDonald's writings are symbolic communications to his friend, the reader. This is true in the double sense that what they refer to (reality as we perceive it) is a symbol and also in that their means of reference (language) is itself, inescapably, symbolic. MacDonald's reader, therefore, must develop 'the power to read the hieroglyphic aspect of things', for he is dealing with an author who believes that literature ought to have as much conscious meaning crammed into it as possible and that, furthermore, any worthwhile piece of literature must have within it much more meaning still, far beyond what the author was conscious of devising.

We have already touched on some of the ways in which MacDonald embeds half-secret meaning in his writing, as when he uses Scots to disguise significance in a proper name. He is far from being the first Scottish novelist to do this, of course, but when he does it, there is often present an extra element of the clandestine. When Galt gives a cheese-producing farmer the surname 'Kibbock', or when Scott calls a schoolmaster 'Whackbairn', the jocular intention indicates that they expect a good proportion of their readers to catch on instantaneously — even many of their English readers. MacDonald's namings seldom have either this openness or this sense of fun. Even when he calls a predatory neighbouring aristocrat 'Lord Lick-my-loof', any fun is swamped by detestation: the name is designed merely to brand a character, not tickle a reader.

It is actually fairly rare for MacDonald to apply this technique to characters: it is his place-names which are often invented thus. The secretness can take the form, as we have seen, of using obscurely regional expressions, as in 'Rothieden', but it is even more frequently a case of using local, specialised knowledge as a springboard. An example would be the naming of the river 'Daur' along which Sir Gibbie's life is lived. Few non-Scots will recognise the word as a Scottish pronunciation of the verb, to 'dare'. Aberdonians, however, may also know that MacDonald is imagining his tale occurring in Aberdeen and in the valley of the Dee, one of Aberdeen's two rivers. One realises with a jolt that MacDonald has seen the real river name as the Scottish verb, to 'do': there is a kind of latent pun, here, which charges a piece of the Scottish landscape with meaning (though without any etymological justification). An even more obscure example of the same process is in his naming of the principal street in the Aberdeen of *Robert Falconer*, 'Pearl Street'. The real street he has in mind is Union Street, named after the union of 1801 of Great Britain and Ireland.[7] Mindful, no doubt, of *Hamlet*, V. 2. 264, however, he has chosen to respond to what is hidden and poetic in the apparently prosaic word.

It is of a piece with his whole sense of the nature of reality that he should use literature to reveal, or at least to play with, the meanings hidden in the world around us, but obscured through our ignorance and dulled awarenesses. His loaded names draw little attention to themselves: 'Rothieden' seems convincingly akin to, say, 'Rothiemurchus', while the English estate on which Hugh Sutherland in *David Elginbrod* has his adventures is the neutral-seeming 'Arnstead' — but the dictionary reveals this to mean 'the place of the Alder', and no reader of Chapter Six of *Phantastes* could believe that this is not significant. High up in the valley of the Daur, Sir Gibbie finds a home in the 'Gormgarnet' mountains: MacDonald clearly has the Cairngorms in mind, and he only half-alters the name. However, the half of the word which is new ('garnet') suggests that he had been thinking of 'cairngorms' as semi-precious stones as much as he thought of them as mountains: the domain in which Gibbie finds love and security is a precious place indeed.

Very occasionally, MacDonald makes meaningful use of the implications of character-names which he has not coined himself: Clementina in *The Marquis of Lossie* really does stand for clemency, while Arctura in *Donal Grant* is indeed a starry being to whom the hero aspires. Malison, in *Alec Forbes*, is a blighting curse on the children of Glamerton. None of these names, however, wear their allegorical status on their sleeves. Nor does Beauchamp when he attains to the clan-chief's title of

The MacChattachan; even less does the howdie in *Malcolm*, Mrs. Catanach, seem significantly named. Yet, early in the novel she is described as 'a cat-wuman', and her name in Gaelic means 'belonging to (Clan) Chattan', a clan which claimed descent from Gillacatain, 'servant of (St.) Catan, "little cat"'.[8] Both these descendants from the servant of the cat are feline in their quiet, sly, hypocritic malevolence, and seem related, in MacDonald's sensibility, to the cat-creatures of *Lilith*.

Such details are interesting in themselves, but their significance lies in MacDonald's sense of the world as a domain containing hidden meanings which the poetic mind can extract and build into literature. Anything which had held his imagination, whether from his reading or from his life, might act as a meaning-carrier and consequently appear, sometimes repeatedly, in his writing. His works are filled with images, characters, situations, patterns, which recur in such a way as to suggest that they held special significance for MacDonald. It is as if, once he felt he had grasped one facet of the great meaning which faces us, he felt justified in offering it in work after work. 'Let our imagination interpretive reveal to us one severed significance of one of her parts, and such is the harmony of the whole, that all the realm of Nature is open to us henceforth'.[9] Hence, his works are full of such repeated symbols as the castles, palaces, cottages, caves, roofs, stairways and libraries that make up the essential landscapes which his heroes and heroines have to negotiate, while tussling with the villainies of sneering aristocrats, seductive, vampire-like sirens and evil embodiments of deadly materialism such as Robert Bruce in *Alec Forbes* and Mrs. Catanach in the Portlossie novels. MacDonald's heroes are aided by the virtuous girls (either of humble origin or oppressed aristocrats) whom they will marry as a sign of union with the divine, but who all need some form of rescue in the course of the tale. Heroes and heroines are variously aided by older mentors, however, in whom part of the divine truth to which the protagonists are growing is embodied — David Elginbrod (and, eventually, his wife), Thomas Crann and Tibbie in *Alec Forbes*, Robert Falconer's grandmother (and grandmothers are even more prominent in the fantasy writing), Janet Grant, who takes in and adopts the waif Sir Gibbie, and many others. Throughout MacDonald's long career as a writer, the same symbolic properties and actions recur: immersion in water, the discovery by a weary traveller of a cosy fireside interior with a warming fire at its centre and a grandmotherly old lady to preside over it, the unravelling and neutralising of an evil secret, the exploration of a labyrinthine interior which often possesses secret stairs and rooms as well as secrets from the past, the dream-like journey through time and over landscapes of the mind, the final resolution and salvation brought about through a combination of human courage and rectitude, and heavenly miracle.

MacDonald's recurrent symbols, however, are not merely embedded, arbitrarily, into narratives which are not themselves symbolic. On the contrary, all his stories, whether overtly fantasy or not, have patterns and implications which point their meaning far beyond the immediate lives of their characters. The handiest term for such symbolic narratives is allegory, which I shall use despite the fact that, in general, it is now almost a term of critical abuse, and despite, furthermore, MacDonald's cautious awareness of how difficult it is to produce a satisfying allegory. It should be no great surprise, however, to find allegory being used by an idealist Victorian novelist for, despite Coleridge, the mode was a widely used resource in Victorian art and expression, as we can see in the work of such poets as

Tennyson and the Pre-Raphaelites, such painters as
Holman Hunt and Madox Brown, and photographers
with ambition to rival painting such as Oscar Rejlander
and Julia Margaret Cameron. In addition, not only
does MacDonald's whole cast of mind tend towards
seeing meaning in all aspects of life, but high amongst
his favourite works of literature were the allegorical *The
Pilgrim's Progress* and *The Faerie Queene.*

The following two chapters of this study deal with
the major fantasies and the fairytales for children,
works which clearly demand discussion in terms of
symbol and, conceivably, of allegory. The remainder of
this chapter will be devoted to exploring some examples
of allegory in the novels. It is hoped that this will not
only illuminate the works themselves, but will further
bring out their kinship with MacDonald's more popular
fantasy work. It will also be an opportunity to bring
out the uniqueness of each novel: it is often implied
that there are no major distinctions to be drawn
between them. Despite obvious broad similarities of
tone, method, outlook, and fictional situations, each
novel is a new departure in mood, thematic emphasis
and imaginative impulse.

In the late *Castle Warlock* (1882), MacDonald's
obvious love of symbolism can be seen growing
outwards to enfold a whole book in allegory. While
lacking the dense and varied evocation of a Scottish
social reality which distinguishes earlier and better
novels, and substituting for this a strong infusion of
gothic romance, this work nevertheless has a surprising
power to move the reader with its vision of the
relentless, wearying encroachment of the world upon
the life of the spirit. The narrative itself carries this
meaning, telling as it does the tale of a family's
progressive loss of all that is important to them —
inherited property, prestige and the power to take care
of dependants, a beloved wife and mother, and

(almost) hope and vitality itself. Reinforcing this tale, however, is the haunting image of the castle itself, symbolising the stunted and threatened inheritance of past family grandeur, which in turn represents threatened Christian hope and belief in an age of Victorian doubt and materialism. The emotion generated by the family plight is far in excess of what the romance surface of the tale seems to demand, and the castle and its situation can be felt carrying broader implications in a manner characteristic of allegory.

This is perhaps most clear at the beginning of Chapter Twenty-one, where the wintry ferocity of the elements is described assailing the house as the laird tries to create some warmth in the draughty old building:

> A sense of fierce desolation, of foreign invasion and siege, took possession of the soul of the laird. He had made a huge fire, and had heaped up beside it a great store of fuel, but, though his body was warm and likely to be warm, his spirit felt the ravaging cold outside — remorseless, and full of mock, the ghastly power of negation, of unmaking. (CW, p. 126; chap. 21, 'That Same Night').

As Grizzie, the servant, says 'The Prence is haein' his ain w'y the nicht' — in other words, the Prince of the Power of the Air (the Devil) has it all his own way. The castle is a defence against the devilish power 'of negation, of unmaking' — against all that is not God, in fact. As such, it stands for faith, both the daily faith of the individual believer, and the ancient faith of a culture or of mankind in general. At the novel's outset, it is described as a 'grim, repellent, unlovely building', 'like the hard-featured face of a Scotch matron, with no end of story, of life, of character, holding a defensive if not defiant front to the world, but within warm, and tending carefully the fires of life' (CW, p. 2; chap. 1,

'Castle Warlock'). Readers of *Robert Falconer* will inevitably remember Robert's grandmother at this point, who is paradoxical in precisely this way and whose outlook has been moulded by the traditional tenets of Calvinism. In this later novel, MacDonald seems to be envisaging his inheritance of traditional Christianity as venerable, ugly and crumbling, yet still to be clung to against all the ravages of Victorian materialism. The castle of Christianity is in more danger, however, of passing from the possession of its rightful owners, than of crumbling within itself. This is probably an oblique comment on how the development of misguided Calvinist doctrine — a logical system which MacDonald saw as a materialistic triumph of the head over the heart — had almost completely usurped the true spirit of Christ within the Church. Indeed, over the centuries, Castle Warlock has developed a strength which leaves little enough space for the humanity it is supposed to preserve:

> In the two [blocks] which stood end to end, hardly a window was to be seen on the side towards the valley; while in the third, which, looking much of the same period, had all its upper part of later origin, were more windows, though none in the ground story. Narrow as were these buildings, and four stories high, they had a solid, ponderous look, suggesting a thickness of the walls such as to leave little of a hollow within for the occupiers; they were like the huge shell built for itself by a small mollusk. (CW, p. 2)

Narrow, high, sturdy, with few outlooks on the immediate world of man and nature but with some recent ones a little nearer to heaven, the castle is sited, as the novel's opening paragraph tells us, 'in debatable land between Highlands and Lowlands; most of its people spoke both Scotch and Gaelic'. Duality continues in the account of the agriculture of the region, for some of the land is bleak, inhospitable, wintry; slopes and valleys facing south, however, are soft and productive. Memories stir of Anodos's encounter with the alder-maiden and the ash tree in *Phantastes* when one reads of 'each glen with its small stream, on the banks of which grew here and there a silver birch, a mountain ash, or an alder tree'. In Scottish folk-lore, the birch, too, has its significance; it is a sacred plant associated with death, as the ballad 'The Wife of Usher's Well' reminds us. At first glance, therefore, MacDonald's description of the castle and the scene of most of the action of the novel seems merely a realistic account of part of the landscape of north-east Scotland. Looked at more closely, it can be seen as an allegorical landscape where Man lives between heights and depths, in a world partly designed for his comfort and partly inhospitable, with elements speaking of spiritual dangers and of death itself. Mankind seems to have a mere foothold in this landscape, apart from the sturdy, ancient, threatened shell of the castle of Christian faith.

At first reading, the opening paragraphs call no attention to themselves as allegory: MacDonald has found all that he needs in that way within the confines of accurate knowledge and observation. Yet enough is done to prepare for a work which will develop the hints of meaning built into the opening description: the essence of the novel is latent in the initial allegorical statement. Few of MacDonald's other novels are built on quite such a concentrated, symbolic image — though *Sir Gibbie*, essentially concerned with the impact of the central Christ-figure on the failings and grubbiness of modern life, has its allegory similarly implicit in its opening scene in which the angelic child searches in the gutter for humanity's lost jewel. This, in turn, illustrates the continuity over many years of images which in MacDonald's mind were clearly packed with central significance, for the opening scene of *Sir Gibbie* is a taking-up of an aside in *Robert Falconer* twelve years before: when Robert considers the possibility of searching for his father, the hopelessness of the task is expressed in 'He might as well search the streets of a great city for a lost jewel' (RF, p. 331; III, 1, 'In the Desert'). *Sir Gibbie*, however, is one of the few Scottish novels to retain some vestigial shreds of reputation among ordinary readers, so to conclude this chapter I shall look at the allegory in certain works which seem to me to be as fine but which are in even more need of advocacy.

Alec Forbes of Howglen is one of these. As in all MacDonald's fictions, the hero of that book can be seen as embodying the essence of mankind. *Alec Forbes* begins with Alec still a juvenile, suggesting that man is child-like in essence but must undergo a phase of moral growth. Alec's progress is a paradigm of essential human growth as MacDonald conceived it, from a childhood perfection of vigorous righteousness, through an adolescent Fall in which he learns his vulnerability to the evils and disappointments of life, until he attains a mature moral security when, at last, he finds God. In plot terms, however, the culmination of that growth is marriage, and the story of Alec's relationship with Annie Anderson is an allegory of mankind's instinct to unite with the perfection of God. MacDonald builds on the Victorian idealisation of woman to create an image of what best we long for: Annie is designed as Alec's Beatrice, and the novel is the tale of his coming to realise this. It is also the tale of Annie's lifelong search for a home, whereby MacDonald articulates his sense of Christ's patient quest for lodgement and acknowledgement within the human breast. When Man recognises, accepts and rejoices in the patient, quiet Christ who has always loved him as Annie has always loved Alec, then Man has the eternal happiness of a fictional bridegroom on the last page of a novel.

Yet Annie is no mere abstract embodiment of divine perfection: we sense a psychological symbiosis between the boy and the girl. While children, they share the same experiences of school and play, but where Annie suffers (at the hands of the Bruces, or in Malison's school) Alec triumphs. To the boy, Glamerton is a glorious playground, despite its flaws; to the girl, it is dark and oppressive. Alec's special care for Annie erupts into various rescues — from water, from snow, from homelessness; and when the boy goes off to university for part of the year, the girl takes his place in his mother's house. There is a dimension of psychodrama here: Annie is an aspect of Alec — that in him which is naturally nearest to God in being sensitive, loving, patient, and wise. Alec keeps saving her because she is his best part; on the other hand, she needs Alec who embodies the vigour, courage and confidence which is also required while we live on Earth. Their final avowed acceptance of each other implies not only a completed moral pattern, but a kind of psychic wholeness, as well.

Nor is it going to far, I think, to interpret the other characters who play major roles in Alec's life as elements in the same psychodrama: Thomas Crann and Cupples are both versions of that within us which guides us with a sense of received authority. They correspond to the 'old men' who appear in some of the fantasy writing — the trio of Old Men in 'The Golden Key' and Mr. Raven/Adam in *Lilith*. Kate Fraser, on the other hand, is the love of the things of the world alone, an impulse which is natural to a young and inexperienced person like Alec, but one which drains because it cannot finally satisfy. Her death by drowning implies the deluded and self-destructive implications of such a love, while Alec's failure to save her (despite his frequent successes in saving Annie) suggest that the worldly, however seductively attractive, cannot be given a home in the affections of mankind at its truest.

That such meanings do not lie on the surface is a sign, not necessarily of over-ingenious interpretation, but of MacDonald's success in following his beloved Spenser (among others) in creating a dark conceit — here, within the romantic realism of a Victorian regional novel. In later works, he is marginally more open in what he is doing, providing at least a clue to the novel's meaning and method. In *Robert Falconer*, for example, he allows an urchin of the slums to articulate the ultimate truth about Robert: 'He's Jesus Christ' (RF, p. 425; III, 11, 'The Suicide'). We could have deduced this anyway from MacDonald's account of Robert's work in the East End, where he cares as much for men's souls as he does for their bodies, and where he gathers around him, with the same natural spontaneity of Jesus's gathering of the disciples, a group of helpers. While this novel appears to follow its predecessor in recounting the growth to manhood of a young Scottish hero, it is significant that, apart from a few comic hints of criticism of the adolescent Robert, the Fall has no place here. Robert never ceases to be as good as he is at the beginning and the end. What changes is the style and scope of his active goodness: it is a boy's goodness at the beginning and a man's at the end — and it is in this final achieved goodness that Christness is apparent.

With Robert identified as Christ, the story of his search for his lost and delinquent father takes on depth. Robert Lee Wolff sees this as the main theme of the novel, and interprets it, along Freudian lines, as deriving from putative guilt feelings in MacDonald as regards his own father.[10] Be that as it may, this strand can be, and probably should be, read as an allegory of Christ, the Son of Man, saving his all-too-human father. The question of the Atonement was central to MacDonald's theological radicalism. Rejecting the orthodox view of Christ's significance as lying in a mysterious substitution of the entirely innocent for (some of) the utterly guilty, MacDonald believed, rather, that men were saved when the Christ in each of them triumphed, and that one of the operations of the triumphant Christ was to strive to call forth the Christ in others. This is the true theme, I believe, of *Robert Falconer*: it is in accord with the emphasis of the narrative surface which is more strongly and continuously concerned with the broad growth of Robert to his full Christlike force than it is with the narrower search for Andrew Falconer. This last, while it provides an important impulse in Robert's development, turns out to be less than his final total achievement. Unlike his theological opponents (and unlike the youthful Robert Falconer himself), MacDonald did not regard salvation, as traditionally conceived, as the ultimate goal at which men should aim; instead, that goal should be the complete acceptance of the will of God — whatever that should be. Thomas Crann, in *Alec Forbes*, comes close to this view, despite himself, when he urges Alec to risk death on a flooded river to save Annie and Tibbie. When Alec pleads fear for the present state of his soul — 'Gin I gang to the boddom, I gang to hell' — Thomas thunders, 'Better be damned, doin' the will o' God, than saved doin' noathing!' (AF, p. 286; chap. 63). Hell, to MacDonald, was no ultimate terror; rather, it was a spiritual detention centre where a sharp shock (short or long depending on the cooperativeness of each inmate soul) would eventually bring about the rehabilitation of every offender into the community of heaven. Hell was thus no longer a state to be avoided at all costs, but rather a somewhat regrettable means towards aligning Man's will with God's. Robert's tale

— like MacDonald's own — is that of the discovery and performance of God's will for him: the 'saving' of his father is an important, but not all-embracing, part of that. While not wishing to deny the general view that the finest parts of *Robert Falconer* are those based on Huntly, I would argue that this is a stronger novel than recent writers have assumed, especially in the satisfying rightness of the narrative form MacDonald has devised to articulate his theme.

This is even more true of the two Scottish novels which followed *Robert Falconer* after a break of several years. *Malcolm* (1875) was continued by that rare thing, a true sequel, in *The Marquis of Lossie* (1877). Together they constitute MacDonald's most extended and elaborate allegory of Christ's triumph, a process which extends even to a version of the Day of Judgement. In these works, MacDonald's imagination recreates the Moray Firth fishing village of Cullen, where he spent several holidays as a child. Here, he sets a version of the standard romance plot of the lost heir: the fisher lad, Malcolm MacPhail, is eventually revealed as the son of the local aristocrat who, twenty years previously, had been tricked into believing that his first wife, Malcolm's mother, had died with her child in childbirth. MacDonald breathes life into this threadbare plot because he believes in it, in a sense: the quotation from *Wilfred Cumbermede* (see above, p. 33) suggests how he saw the fantasy of high birth as evidence for the instinct within men to reattain their heavenly birthright.

Malcolm's true identity is revealed to himself, to the reader, and to a few other characters at the end of *Malcolm*, but is not proclaimed to the world until the end of the sequel. This is so that Malcolm can imitate the operation of Christ within each of us by trying to persuade the flighty half-sister whom he loves (the embodiment of fallen humanity), to a wiser course of life and to a state of mind in which she can accept her inevitable loss of rank: unknown to her, she is the illegitimate offspring of their father. In fact, only the undeniable revelation of Malcolm's right can induce the childishly stubborn Florimel to give up her wilful insistence on her own independence, but once Malcolm assumes command of the family estates he is able to mete out reward and punishment and establish a securely happy patriarchal despotism — somewhat along the lines of MacDonald's notion of true clan-chieftanship. As we read this quaint but impressive climax to the great double work, we sense MacDonald's tale touching, on one side, on the process of Christ's triumph within each of us and, on the other, illuminating the meaning of the doctrine of the Judgement Day itself.

In case we miss Malcolm's significance, MacDonald has his 'grandfather', the seer-like blind piper Duncan MacPhail, worry over a couple of wounds which the young fisherman sustains in the course of the plot: 'Wownded in ta hand and in ta foot!... What can it mean? It must mean something, Malcolm, my son' (M, p. 260; chap. 42, 'Duncan's Disclosure'). It means, of course, that Malcolm is already to be seen as Christ-like, even at this fairly early stage in the plot. With this novel, MacDonald moved from concentrating on the tale of how we all gradually grow more like Christ, to one in which the Christ element is visible and active (in the guise of the energetic young hero) right from the beginning. *Bildungsroman* gives way to the tale of the lost heir; allegorical psychodrama gives place to a yet more committed allegorical method. This comes about partly because the story of our growth to Christlikeness has now been thoroughly told in the earlier novels, but also because MacDonald's vision seems to be undergoing a subtle shift. To portray the emergence of Christ within us as a steady, natural growth, despite the impediments the world puts in the way, is to offer a vision of glowing optimism: it stresses inevitability and tends to play down the difficulties within the process. Thus, the pain in the world of *Alec Forbes* seems, in our recollections, more superficial than its happiness and serenity. The bleakness of atmosphere in *Robert Falconer*, in retrospect, heralds a change: it is as if MacDonald were taking the difficulties of the world with greater seriousness than ever before. His growing respect for evil induced him, in *Malcolm*, to abandon the narrative model he had adopted hitherto: henceforth, his task was to show good and evil locked in permanent opposition.

The spirit of conflict, therefore, becomes a guiding principle in the Portlossie novels. It is given a symbol in the meaning which Malcolm, in his poetical way, ascribes to the sunset flaming over the fishing fleet: 'It's the battle o' Armageddon...the battle atween the richt and the wrang, 'at ye read aboot i' the buik o' the Revelations' (M, p. 135; chap. 23, 'Armageddon'). MacDonald's previous novels had not lacked a sense of opposition between right and wrong, sometimes precipitating in scenes of charged conflict between characters. These confrontations, usually verbal, though occasionally physical, and filled with a moral anger which undoubtedly derives from MacDonald's own temperament, invite the reader's emotional participation on the side of right. In *Malcolm*, however, conflict occurs to a quite remarkable extent: incidents of physical violence alone, involving humans or animals, number fifteen (ranging from a scuffle between pupils in the schoolroom to the dirking of Malcolm's hand). On top of this, there are many scenes in which indignation, anger and denial dominate: characters swiftly become adversaries. Conversations now take on a confrontational quality which they had less frequently in earlier novels, with the result that they make charged, gripping reading.

Other kinds of tension appear, too. In many of

MacDonald's novels, heroes are emotionally teased and played with by upper-class flirts, but the early scenes in which Florimel first encounters the young fisherman have a dramatic solidity and a clear sexuality which takes us by surprise. Dialectic appears to have become the characteristic working mode of MacDonald's mind: even when he is describing and evaluating the little religious revival which springs up amongst the fisher-folk, his account oscillates between pro and con until a full, balanced and complex assessment has been reached.

The tense balance of a confrontation of opposites runs deep, here. The poise of MacDonald's response to the revival is matched by his wise even-handedness in describing the culture of the fisher-folk: 'Their women were in general coarse in manners and rude in speech; often of great strength and courage, and of strongly-marked character... I may add that, although [a fisher-wife's] eldest child was probably born within a few weeks after her marriage, infidelity was almost unknown amongst them' (M, p. 11; chap. 4, 'Phemy Mair'). Furthermore, even the explosive impulse to righteous anger, and the book's apparent refusal to compromise with evil, is balanced by a thoughtfulness on the morality of this very attitude. (C. S. Lewis, for one, became rather uneasy about the moral, as well as the artistic, healthiness of the explosions of indignation in MacDonald's novels).[11] MacDonald ponders these considerations in the person of Malcolm's grandfather, the blind piper, who is endowed with an abiding hatred of Campbells, thanks to their treachery at Glencoe. He is made to rethink his violent and indiscriminate detestation after he wounds his grandson, thinking him to be a Campbell and the perpetrator of a cruel practical joke. Through Duncan, MacDonald draws a distinction between the justified, morally reliable spontaneity of momentary anger, and a settled, cold, ruthless vindictiveness.

Above all, balance is found in the weighting of
initiative between good and evil in the two books as a
whole. In *Malcolm*, evil has the initiative, so that the
tale is of the good characters fending off various assaults
on their welfare and integrity. In *The Marquis of Lossie*,
on the other hand, the flow of action is reversed:
Malcolm now knows who he is and it is he, rather than
the wicked characters, whose plots control the initiative.
The question is not whether good will prevail, but how
it will do so.

The confident aggressiveness of goodness is summed
up by a surprising image that we encounter in a most
unlikely scene. It is provided by Malcolm's mentor, the
dismissed teacher Alexander Graham, whom we find
struggling through the London rain to preach in the
depressing context of a mid-week prayer-meeting in a
Dissenting chapel:

> 'Here I am', he said to himself, 'lance in hand,
> spurring to meet my dragon!'
> Once when he used a similar expression,
> Malcolm had asked him what he meant by his
> dragon; 'I mean', replied the schoolmaster, 'that
> huge slug, *The Commonplace*. It is the wearifulest
> dragon to fight in the whole miscreation'. (ML, p.
> 110; chap. 27, 'The Preacher')

The Spenserian image of principled and ultimately
victorious violence sums up much of the spirit of the
Portlossie novels. It also underlines their use of allegory.
Florimel passes the hours by trying to make something
of *The Faerie Queene*, having discovered that her own
name occurs in it. Spenser's Florimell is a dual
creature: the true, living and virtuous Florimell is
impersonated by a false, empty creature created from
snow by an evil magician. MacDonald's heroine has a
similar duality of worth and behaviour which is
explicitly related to Spenser's allegory in an early scene

between her and Malcolm, on the shore:

> And as he spoke, he gently stretched himself on the
> dune, about three yards aside and lower down.
> Florimel looked half amused and half annoyed, but
> she had brought it on herself, and would punish
> him only by dropping her eyes again on her book,
> and keeping silent. She had come to the Florimel
> of snow. (M, p. 82; chap. 15, 'The Slope of the
> Dune')

In Spenser's Book Three, also, we find in the tale of
Belphoebe and Amoretta two siblings born under
peculiar circumstances and brought up separately so
that marked differences appear. An even more
pronounced indebtedness lies in the fact that Malcolm
was found by Duncan MacPhail, as a newly-born
infant, abandoned in the cave by the sea. In Spenser,
Florimell's beloved is Marinell, son of a mortal man
and a sea nymph:

> There he this knight of her begot, whom borne
>   She of his father *Marinell* did name,
>   And in a rocky cave as wight forlorne,
>   Long time she fostered up, ... (FQ, III. 4.20.1–4)

If Malcolm, therefore, is an embodiment of Christ
who is presented in this case as a Spenserian knight,
and Florimel represents a lovable but often erring
Humanity which pridefully conceives that its status and
importance is higher than it is in reality, then the other
major characters can be assigned similar roles in the
allegorical scheme. Malcolm's father, the Marquis, a
cynical and flawed product of the Regency, is another
embodiment of Humanity: like Robert Falconer's father
Andrew, he is the erring parent of the Son of Man and
most of his faults seem to have been the result of a loss
of contact with the true rightness of things when he lost
(as he thought) his beloved wife. In other words, his

unbelief arose when his heavenward instincts were
thwarted: it is from this attitude that the discovery of
his son eventually saves him. Yet another facet of
mankind is embodied in Duncan MacPhail: he is that
in Humanity which loves and nurtures the child-like
Christ within us all. Like the marquis, he is fallable and
flawed, but his love provides a home in which
Christlikeness can grow to its full power. Evil is
embodied in Mrs. Catanach, the howdie who also helps
lay out the community's corpses: encountered at each
end of life's passage, she clearly embodies Man's mortal
limitations. The tale is of how she had attempted to
thwart Malcolm–Christ's rights by smuggling him away
from the castle of his fathers at the hour of his birth.
Our mortal nature is essentially at odds with our
divinity, and MacDonald imagines it scheming to trick
us out of our rights as God's children.

Mrs. Catanach is the mortal means whereby this
wicked end is attempted; the impetus to bring this
about — the principle which enlists mortality to
obscure our true nature — is embodied in Mrs.
Stewart, the mother of a hunchback, dwarfish, 'mad'
laird, Stephen Stewart. The latter is yet another
embodiment of Humanity, this time seen as a
pathetically limited, twisted, vulnerable falling-off from
the ideal creature God envisaged. Hating and rejecting
his mother, the mad laird lives as he may, relying on
the countryside and the goodwill of ordinary folk to
supply his needs. His obsession — and it is one of the
basic concerns of the novel — is with origins. His cry of
'I dinna ken whaur I come frae!' is the puzzled
expression of humanity's inability to accept its apparent
origins — the purely material origins represented by
Mrs. Stewart — while failing to make out the higher
spiritual source for which it yearns. Mrs. Stewart, a
near neighbour with whom the marquis is rather
blindly on good terms, treats this unfortunate son

cruelly and has him hunted through the countryside
when he escapes. She also lays claim to being the
mother of Malcolm, a possibility he instinctively
discounts: his strong divinity rejects the notion that he
could be the offspring of such a materialist. The
hackneyed tale of the lost heir, therefore, provides the
framework for a complex allegory of the struggle
between the forces of good and evil to possess a
mankind made vulnerable by the obscure and
paradoxical cosmic situation in which it finds itself.
Malcolm's ending on the achievement of knowledge
rather than on the assumption of power is thus
appropriate.

Its sequel, on the other hand, moves towards
Malcolm–Christ's public assumption of authority, but
that revelation, always at hand throughout the action
of *The Marquis of Lossie*, is postponed for as long as
possible. If *Malcolm* is all about the striving for firm
knowledge of Man's heavenly origins, the sequel is
concerned with the striving of the Christ within us to
rectify the human will to accord with God's. Malcolm
tries to encourage the better nature of his sister to assert
itself before he imposes his will on her: in plot terms, he
tries to detach her from the worldly ways of her
London friends and to foster that best self which the
pastoral retreat of Portlossie brings out. Yet, a crucial
part of MacDonald's point is that when Christ strives
to master the human will it is for humanity's sake that
he does so. Hence the tale of his loving struggle to curb
the powerful, magnificent horse Kelpie — like Florimel,
a favourite of his father's — despite the apparent
cruelty involved. Kelpie's spirit and strength are clearly
relished by MacDonald, as we can see in the splendid
account of Malcolm's exercising of the horse on the
seashore (ML, pp. 170–72; chap. 39, 'Discipline').
Kelpie stands for Humanity possessed of a powerful
will, but the freakish impulses of the horse, combined

with its great strength, render it dangerous. Furthermore, it is vulnerable to destruction by those who, lacking Malcolm's love, skill and patience, are endangered by it; this is as much to be feared as the danger the will can inflict on others, for it is no part of the Christian scheme to do away with Man's independent will.

Kelpie is a splendid character, and she is as much a key symbol in the sequel as the Armageddon-like sunset was in *Malcolm*. We may feel that the tale of the foolish misplaced outrage of Lady Clementina as she beholds Malcolm's firmness with the horse is a slipping into the kind of obvious allegorical texturing which many since Coleridge have mistrusted in the form. Nevertheless, Clementina's final union with Malcolm is no mere superficial endgame to tie up the plot: their eventual partnership is necessary. Malcolm ends as a figure of power who can seem ruthless in his final insistence that right must prevail: the dividing-line between getting Florimel to accept his view of things by spelling out the painful truth of her position, and simply imposing his will on her, is very narrow. As in *David Elginbrod* and *Alec Forbes*, they all live happily ever after, but in the earlier works that happiness had seemed based on MacDonald's belief that once all difficulties and misunderstandings had been cleared away, a naturally good mankind would lead a virtuous and happy existence. In these novels of the 1870s, however, the condition which ensures perpetual happiness for God's creatures depends, not on man's inherent goodness but, rather, on the divine attributes of acknowledged power and clemency. The sense that man needs clemency represents a marginal darkening of MacDonald's outlook — a darkening which becomes yet more obvious in later and poorer novels, and also in his fairy writing for adults and for children.

NOTES

1. George MacDonald, *A Dish of Orts*, London, 1893, pp. 58; 18; 5.
2. *A Dish of Orts*, p. 223.
3. S. T. Coleridge, *Biographia Literaria*, 2nd ed., ed. G. Watson, London and New York, 1965, p. 167.; *A Dish of Orts*, p. 28.
4. George MacDonald, *A Book of Strife in the form of The Diary of an Old Soul*, London, 1905, p. 21 ('February' 2, 4).
5. George MacDonald, *At the Back of the North Wind*, New York, 1950, p. 61 (chap. 5, 'The Summer-House').
6. *A Dish of Orts*, p. 8.
7. Fenton Wyness, *City by the Grey North Sea: Aberdeen*, 2nd ed., Aberdeen, 1972, p. 220.
8. P. H. Reaney, *A Dictionary of British Surnames*, 2nd ed., revised by R. M. Wilson, London, 1977, p. 67.
9. *A Dish of Orts*, pp. 18–19.
10. Robert Lee Wolff, *The Golden Key: A Study of the Fiction of George MacDonald*, New Haven, 1961, pp. 230–35.
11. Roger Lancelyn Green & Walter Hooper, *C. S. Lewis: A Biography*, London, 1974, p. 114.

CHAPTER 4

PHANTASTES AND *LILITH*

If any single work of MacDonald's has a claim on the attention of posterity, that work is surely *Phantastes*, his first major piece of prose fiction. Written rapidly, in two months at the end of 1857, it was published in October 1858 with the subtitle, 'A Faerie Romance for Men and Women'. This is itself enough to hint distantly at Spenser's influence, and a glance at the many mottoes and quotations which MacDonald bestows on his chapters reveals that the work grew not only from a fertile interest in German and English romantic writing (Novalis, Goethe, Fouque; Schiller, Heine, Jean Paul, Schleiermacher, Shelley, Wordsworth, Coleridge, Beddoes), but also from a considerable know-ledge of the English Renaissance (Spenser, Fletcher, Tourneur, Shakespeare, Suckling, Lyly, Cowley, Sidney, Decker) as well as Chaucer, ballads, and the Bible.

The strange title is helpful. 'Phantastes' is a character in a poem by one of Spenser's imitators, 'The Purple Island' by Phineas Fletcher, and is the embodiment of 'the fancie' — the mind's fecund capacity to invent ideas and to clothe them in attractive imagery. MacDonald misquotes two lines of this poem on the title-page. The entire stanza from which they come is as follows:

> *Phantastes* from the first all shapes deriving,
> In new abiliments can quickly dight;
> Of all materiall and grosse parts depriving,
> Fits them unto the noble Princes sight;

> Which soon as he hath view'd with searching
> eye,
>   He straight commits them to his Treasurie,
>   Which old *Eumnestes* keeps, Father of memorie.
>   (Canto 6, st. 48)[1]

(MacDonald's substitution of 'their fount' for 'the first' was conceivably intended to bring out more clearly what he took to be the essential meaning Fletcher intended, namely that man's thoughts all derive from the divine fountainhead.) The poem's elaborate allegory is an anatomy of 'the isle of man', and 'the noble Prince' is the Intellect or Understanding. Phantastes is the second of the three chief counsellors of this 'highest Soveraigne' and so a faculty of immense importance and responsibility. MacDonald's implication, therefore, is that this book, a product of the fancy, is not merely, or primarily, written for an outside reader, but is a manifestation of a process going on within its creator himself. Phantastes is part of the means whereby the individual accumulates knowledge and experience. His presence is a sign that an inner growth is taking place, irrespective of outside observers, and his function is to provide the material which the memory stores once the understanding has vetted it. Memory, as we shall see, is a central thematic and structural element: the chapter mottoes alone indicate that MacDonald's mind was full of memories of other literature as he composed the work. Furthermore, it is hard not to believe that in this tale of how Anodos (whose name has several facets of meaning, but whose root meaning seems to be 'the pathless one') wanders through a bewildering Fairyland until he finds a purpose to give him direction, MacDonald is not also remembering the false starts and changes of direction in his own first thirty-three years.

Despite its being rich in literary roots, *Phantastes* strikes readers with its originality, even when they are ignorant of the work's importance as a landmark in the tradition of modern fantasy. Its formal innovations are less important in its appeal, however, than the enduring quality of imaginative freshness which pervades it. The heart of MacDonald's success lies in the quality of imagination which created the landscape of Fairyland and devised the adventures which Anodos encounters within it. The over-riding impression is of a startling fecundity of invention from which pours a tale pleasing to the mind's eye, bewilderingly at odds with our sense of reality, yet harmonious with a lurking coherence and weighted with a convincing moral seriousness. MacDonald's formal starting-point is the German *marchen* as practised by Novalis, Fouque and Hoffman, but the quality of many of his episodes derives much from his English sources (one of which, although not represented by a chapter-motto, is assuredly *A Pilgrim's Progress*), while the basic imaginative texture is provided by the dream. This dream-vision, at first reading, seems fully to attain the Novalis-inspired goal of bewildering incoherence. Nevertheless, its landscape is, throughout, a projection of Anodos's mood and his degree of insight: at first the impression is of abundant colour and vitality in a living forest, but as he accumulates experiences of terror and disappointment, the glowing forest gives way to bleaker landscapes of cave, desolate shore and grim, level moor. This Fairyland is peopled by goblins, witches, malevolent creatures of various kinds, and by Anodos's mysterious Shadow, as well as by more normal mortals who all, nevertheless, derive as much from the traditions of the fairytale as they do from everyday life. Time and again, MacDonald invents a character or situation which strikes us with the power of an archetype. Overt references to Christianity are shunned (even though readers with a wide knowledge of MacDonald's beliefs and other writings will find echoes of them on many of its pages). MacDonald is completely successful in devising a book which lives up to his ideal of the fairy-tale: it has its own clear harmony of imaginative and moral integrity, while remaining open to every reader to develop his own interpretation. Of all his full-length works of fiction, this is the one with the greatest ability to please both with its imaginative quality, and with the conviction with which the achieved form lives up to the apparent intention.

It can seem fruitless to speculate on what prompted this radical innovation in British fiction. Nevertheless, *Phantastes* may perhaps be, in part at least, a response to a recently encountered stimulus. Conjecture rules here, but in the description of the nadir of Anodos's fortunes, when he finds himself on the desolate seashore, we may have a recollection of Arnold's 'Dover Beach'.

> I stood on the shore of a wintry sea, with a wintry sun just a few feet above its horizon-edge. It was bare, and waste, and gray. Hundreds of hopeless waves rushed constantly shorewards, falling exhausted upon a beach of great loose stones, that seemed to stretch miles and miles in both directions. There was nothing for the eye but mingling shades of gray; nothing for the ear but the rush of the coming, the roar of the breaking, and the moan of the retreating wave. No rock lifted up a sheltering severity above the dreariness around ... I wandered over the stones, up and down the beach, a human imbodiment of the nature around me. The wind increased; its keen waves flowed through my soul; the foam rushed higher up the stones; a few dead stars began to gleam in the east; the sound of the waves grew louder and yet more despairing. (p. 127)[2]

At this point, MacDonald's novel shares a bleakness comparable with Arnold's, and uses similar imagery and language to express it. A further similarity is between the openings of the two works. Just as Arnold's speaker is at a window looking out over an attractive nocturnal seascape, which puts him in mind of the Sea of Faith, so Anodos comes round from the swoon induced by his 'grandmother's' gaze and finds himself beholding a scene like Arnold's at Dover: 'I forgot all the rest, till I found myself at the window, whose gloomy curtains were withdrawn, and where I stood gazing on a whole heaven of stars, small and sparkling in the moonlight. Below lay a sea, still as death and hoary in the moon, sweeping into bays and around capes and islands, away, away, I knew not whither. Alas! it was no sea, but a low fog burnished by the moon. 'Surely there is such a sea somewhere!' said I to myself. A low sweet voice beside me replied–

'In Fairy Land, Anodos' (p. 18).

'Dover Beach' was not published until 1867, ten years after *Phantastes* was written. Arnold had written it, however, in the early 1850s (probably late June 1851); were MacDonald to have seen it, therefore, he would have to have been shown it in manuscript.[3] We do not know that this happened but it is certainly possible, for Greville records that by 1859 Arnold knew the MacDonalds — indeed, he 'ranked among their intimates' (GMDW, p. 300) — and the association seems to have lasted at least into the early 1870s (GMDW, p. 412). The outlook expressed in the poem is very different from MacDonald's characteristic optimism, of course, though from his student days MacDonald had associated dreary sea-shores with moods of depression (GMDW, p. 80). Arnold's poem moves from the view of the sea from the window, to a consciousness of 'the eternal note of sadness' in the nature of things, a sadness exacerbated for his generation by the loss of faith. He admits that the world 'seems/To lie before us like a land of dreams' but

Hath really neither joy, nor love, nor light,
Nor certitude, nor peace, nor help for pain.

And he concludes with his famous metaphor of the darkling plain and the ignorant armies. It is a poem without metaphysical hope. Even if this conjecture is wrong, and MacDonald had not yet glimpsed the famous poem, Arnold nevertheless gives us later readers a profound distillation of the mood against which *Phantastes* is directed.

MacDonald also starts with a seascape seen from a window, but proceeds to test the world's dream-like promise with a thoroughness which never occurs to Arnold. As his exploration of the world as dream progresses, Anodos becomes aware, to the full, of sadness: indeed, his journey is an accumulation of disappointments and thwarted longing, but whereas Arnold's poem lets despair prevail, MacDonald's novel places sadness in a larger context in which it is less than final. For MacDonald, despair on the sea-shore is not the cul-de-sac it seems; Anodos positively accepts unhappiness when he plunges into the sea, an act which is immediately rewarded by his finding a little rainbow-coloured boat, which can only signify Hope and which carries him to the cottage on the isthmus. There he finds an old woman who not only provides him with the joy, the love, the light, the certitude, the peace and the help for pain which he immediately needs and which Arnold denies, but, in his subsequent forays into other areas of his life reached by passing through the doors of the cottage, he finds that this haven is always merely a doorway away in the midst of all life's pain. Where Arnold's final consciousness in 'Dover Beach' is of groping across that terrifying plain, Anodo's last thoughts are of the comforting recollection of the wise woman: 'When I am oppressed by any sorrow or real perplexity, I often feel as if I had only

left her cottage for a time, and would soon return out
of the vision, into it again' (p. 182).

MacDonald's aim is clearly not to deny 'the eternal
note of sadness' — indeed, his book is full of it. His
attitude is quite different from Arnold's, however, and
he appears to welcome it in birdsong: 'As in all sweetest
music, a tinge of sadness was in every note. Nor do we
know how much of the pleasures even of life we owe to
the intermingled sorrows. Joy cannot unfold the deepest
truths, although deepest truth must be deepest joy.
Cometh white-robed Sorrow, stooping and wan, and
flingeth wide the doors she may not enter' (pp. 73–74).
This insight immediately precedes his arrival at the
palace of white marble, which turns out to be a kind of
Palace of Art, and where his second crucial discovery of
his White Lady as a work of art — a statue — will take
place. It is as if his new poised insight into the real
meaning of sadness had now equipped him for a deeper
experience of art.

It seems significant, also, that his capacity to hear
the sadness in the birdsong occurs very soon after he
has acquired his Shadow. As most commentators agree,
the Shadow is a symbol of many facets, but the variety
of detailed interpretations which have been offered is
worrying: we are told that it means such things as guilt,
worldly-wise cynicism and dissillusionment, self-
centredness, intellectuality and materialism, loss of
innocence and optimism, and many more. This is in
stark contrast to the implication of the ogre (in whose
house Anodos acquires his shadow) that there is a
single label for it: 'I believe you call it by a different
name in your world' (p. 64). What name does
MacDonald have in mind? Chapter Nine is devoted to
the blighting effects of the shadow on Anodos's
behaviour, attitudes and surroundings. That chapter
has, as a motto, a few lines from Coleridge's 'Dejection:
An Ode' (11.47–9; 53–8), in which the source of the

world's life and beauty — but also of its deadness and emptiness — is seen as lying within us: 'Ours is her wedding garment, ours her shroud!' Anodos's shadow seems to be MacDonald's version of Coleridge's *Dejection*, and it is notable that in all the shadow's later comings and goings, Anodos's mood seems to be the triggering factor. Thus, the strange reappearance of the shadow immediately after the fight with the giants, where we might have expected Anodos to exult after surviving a worthy battle, is the embodiment of that depression which can so easily afflict us when we relax after a mighty effort. When Anodos says finally that he has come back 'rejoicing that I had lost my Shadow', what he has lost is that capacity for despair which is death to our ability to see the world as lying before us like a land of dreams.

His first loss of the shadow occurs in the fairy palace, where his denunciation of it causes the landscape to be flooded with sunlight 'as with a silent shout of joy' (p. 78). Similarly, 'joy' is the keyword which echoes three times through the six lines succeeding his final realisation that his shadow has left him (p. 181). Coleridge's great antidote to *Dejection* is clearly MacDonald's counterpoise to the shadow, and his novel can be seen as an exploration of the eternal struggle between Joy and Dejection, to see which is the more fundamental. But whereas joy is the first of the elements which Arnold denies at the climax of his poem, it is the prevailing mood which finally ushers Anodos home. Joy does indeed exist, despite Arnold, to clear away Dejection, and leave untramelled 'the eternal note of sadness' which flings open the doors to the deepest truth: as a result of his experiences, Anodos is always reminded by sorrow of the wise woman in the cottage, with her words of comforting assurance, 'A great good is coming to thee'.

To emphasise the theme of sadness and joy as a key

to the book is not to deny the importance of other interpretations which have been placed upon it. Thus, Colin Manlove has eloquently described it as 'concerning itself with the First Things, and with true birth, self-realisation and movement into the world', while Roland Hein stresses the loss of self, and David Holbrook the urge to reunite with the lost Mother (a reflection of MacDonald's own early loss of his mother).[4] The reader can find all these and other ways of understanding *Phantastes*, for it is particularly rich in interpretative possibilities and would seem to embody MacDonald's own belief that a fairytale ought to be open to whatever meaning each reader can find in it. MacDonald certainly believed that no meaning should be imposed on a fairytale by its author, and that the artist's unconscious should be free from the dictates of the rational, materialist part of his mind. In such circumstances, the creative impulse would be most open to the promptings of God, and the resulting work as near as could be to an embodiment of God's truth. Hence his substantial quotation from Novalis, which acts as a kind of preface. Part of this can be translated: 'A fairy story is like a disjointed dream-vision, an ensemble of wonderful things and occurrences, for example, a musical fantasy, the harmonic sequences of an Aeolian harp, nature itself...'

In a sense, the book lives up to this prescription, but not completely. It is impossible to believe that MacDonald's unconscious enjoyed untrammelled sway, for many episodes seem to contain a firmness of intention which their lack of surface explicitness cannot conceal. Thus, Anodos's concluding adventure in Fairyland, his self-sacrificing exposure of the destruction at the heart of the great ceremonial in the twenty-third chapter, is usually taken as reflecting the author's own antagonism to the prevailing religious orthodoxy. Occasionally, too, MacDonald's allegorical instinct

peeps through, as when, during the desolate under-
ground journey following the second loss of the White
Lady (a journey in which Anodos encounters, and
shrugs off, the torments of goblins), Anodos's state of
mind is explored in terms of allegorical abstractions.
'Besides being delighted and proud that *my* songs had
called the beautiful creature to life, the same fact
caused me to feel a tenderness unspeakable for her,
accompanied with a kind of feeling of property in her;
for so the goblin Selfishness would reward the angel
Love' (p. 126).

C. S. Lewis's formulation, that MacDonald's fantasy
'hovers between the allegorical and the mythopoeic'
seems an excellent statement of the mixture of conscious
control and mysterious imaginative spontaneity which
Phantastes presents.[5] It is both a mental wonderland
with an appeal which, in part, brings out the childlike
in each sympathetic reader while, at the same time, it is
an elaborate organisation of symbols which perpetually
tease us to interpretation. Yet the impulse to allegorise,
to decode meanings which then, as it were, *supercede*
their narrative source, seems particularly insensitive in
the case of such a work as this, in which the imagined
narrative is of such prominence and attractiveness.

In fact, the 'world' which is *Phantastes* is no mere
means to an end. The book itself contains suggestions
that the sheer experience of entering the domain which
MacDonald's imagination has created is the heart of
what the book has to offer. For example, Hein is right
to stress the loss of self as a theme, but his account
veers towards presenting this as a moral which is to be
taken, as it were, from a reading. This is in the tradition
of C. S. Lewis's view that MacDonald's genius is such
that 'its connection with words at all turns out to be
merely external and, in a sense, accidental'.[6] In fact,
this is never true of MacDonald at his best, and least
of all is it true of *Phantastes*, which rewards in

corresponding measure however much attention we pay to the details of verbal expression and formal structuring. Thus, while we may, if we like, describe the work as an illustration 'that it is better to serve others than ourselves, and that our desires can be satisfied indirectly through this service', it seems more true to our experience of reading it to stress how both Anodos and the reader grow, unsuspectingly, into that loss of self which can be described as entering another world.[7]

The process of Anodos learning to lose himself, however, is not completed until late in the narrative — if, indeed, it is really completed within the narrative of his Fairyland journey at all. Even his final ejection from Fairyland seems due to a sudden resurgence of self, or of pride. Having apparently attained to the acme of selflessness in giving his 'life' to destroy the evil ceremony, and thereafter enjoying death as an afterlife of service to others, he finds himself floating on a cloud, like a god, over a great city. Looking down at toiling humanity, he exclaims, 'O pale-faced women, and gloomy-browed men, and forgotten children, how I will wait on you, and minister to you, and, putting my arms about you in the dark, think hope unto your hearts, when you fancy no one is near! Soon as my senses have all come back, and have grown accustomed to this new blessed life, I will be among you with the love that healeth' (pp. 179–80). In this moment of supreme giving, he seems to even himself with Christ: with supreme insight, MacDonald *creates* the limits of human perfection by an ultimate ambiguity. Is the ejection from Fairyland, which seems a consequence of this exclamation, a sign that the final moral benefit of Anodos's fairy journey has been reaped, or is it a punishment for allowing self to enter in the moment of ultimate selflessness? 'With this, a pang and a terrible shudder went through me; a writhing as of death convulsed me; and I became once again conscious of a more limited, even a bodily and earthly life' (p. 180). Are these birth-pangs a reward or a penalty?

And just as the struggle between self and selflessness is still being played out at the end, so, at the outset (when, in many interpretations, Anodos has not even started on his moral journey) he is already showing the first signs of that capacity for selflessness which eventually become a conscious ideal in him. For what else is his initial curiosity about his father's story, and his regarding of the contents of the secretary as 'this long-hidden world', but an instinct to explore the world of the non-self? Curiosity, or the desire to appropriate the outlook of another, is merely an inferior degree of that union of self-giving and self-glory which causes his final return to each. Similarly, such moments as his encounter with the beech tree (whom he quits with some sense of guilt as well as with the knowledge that their encounter has given her something valuable) and his two releases of the White Lady (which are a giving of life to her, but also spring from a selfish desire to possess her) continue the meditation on man's entrapment in the net woven by the nearly related threads of his selfishness and selflessness. Accounts of the book which reduce it to a tale of simple moral education reduce its subtlety.

Nevertheless, there is a progress in the book in terms of the deepening of Anodos's understanding of the issues, and of his desire for moral improvement. And in this deepening, his willingness to enter world after world is a key factor. Thus his entry into the world of the secretary is followed by his impulse to encounter the sea glimpsed from the window, then by his willingness to accept, without the surprise which is the result of judging by one's familiar expectations, all the strange events Fairyland has to offer. It continues with, in particular, his willingness to share the task of the two princes and his acceptance of brotherhood with them. Furthermore, he develops an insatiable appetite for the worlds proffered by the many works of literature he encounters in his travels. Such moments reveal what is positive in him, but they are always succeeded, sooner or later, by phases of self-centredness. The alternation is the heartbeat of life itself.

What MacDonald understands so well about such a theme as self and selfishness is not so much told to us, however, as enshrined in the book's structure, or even in its very nature. If MacDonald's habitual note of didacticism is not entirely banished, it is reduced almost to nothingness, partly because the narrative is in the first person. Consequently, the moral explicitness, when it occurs, is Anodos's, rather than MacDonald's. This point is no mere critical sleight-of-hand: the choice of narrative person is a function of that avoidance of the personality of the historical author which so crucially sets *Phantastes* and *Lilith* apart from the rest of MacDonald's fiction. Fantasy, especially as MacDonald creates it here, is a less than explicit medium. In writing the work, MacDonald is giving the Phantastes within him its head: a part, at least, of the benefit of the creation of the book lies in the enrichment of his own 'noble Prince' (his understanding) as a result of the insights gained during its creation and stored in his memory. Indeed, if *Phantastes* is, as I suspect, in part a debate with the outlook Arnold expresses in 'Dover Beach', then the fact that the poem was not public property would mean that MacDonald's work has, more than ever, a private dimension which has not hitherto been suspected.

If this is so, then *Phantastes* is a work of art with an important role to play in the life of its author as well as (MacDonald must have hoped) the lives of its readers. It is one of the surprises which define Anodos's Fairyland that art and life exist on equal and interchangeable terms. The note is sounded at the outset, as Anodos muses on how his father 'had woven his web of story' and as the fairy grandmother promises that Anodos will enter the fairyland for which he had yearned when he read a fairytale to his little sister. His White Lady, whom he releases from encasement in the alabaster block by means of his singing, is, in one sense, the living work of art which he has created — an interpretation strengthened by her later preference for remaining as a statue in an art gallery. One of the most important characters, the knight Sir Percival, is first encountered in a book read by Anodos in the cottage which provides him with his first refuge in Fairyland, and the manifold tales and poems embedded in the narrative all interact with, and reflect, the main story in a number of ways. The world of art — and especially its literary subdivision — is a constant and equal presence alongside the more obviously living constituents of the fairy country. What Anodos learns and experiences in literature is of comparable moment with any of his other encounters. Indeed, Anodos is quite explicit in this matter: in summarising his voluminous reading in the library of the fairy palace, he describes how he entered fully into whatever book he read, identifying with it completely. 'Mine was the whole story' (p. 81).

The implication is clear both that a human life is a tale and that what one finds within the covers of a book can be as vital a part of one's understanding of reality as anything encountered in 'real life'. And equally clear is the implication, for MacDonald's reader, that this general truth is especially true of the particular book he holds in his hand. Not only do numerous incidents illustrate the interfusion of life and literature, but at many points literature is shown having an effect in the world around it: the tale of Sir Percival is a warning against the Maid of the Alder;

Anodos's songs twice reveal and release the White Lady; the Wise Woman's songs soothe Anodos's distress; Anodos sings to the brother princes songs which make them weep but which consequently strengthen them; the maid of the globe releases Anodos from the dreary tower by her singing (as she says, 'wherever I go, my songs do good, and deliver people' — p. 163); even the sight of a child reading helps Anodos to believe in Fairyland once again.

It is clear, too, that memories of other literature have been crucial in helping form *Phantastes*: an awareness of sources does not merely help us explain the work's genesis, but can conceivably take us to the heart of it. This applies even to the chapter-mottoes, which are much more intimately related to the rest of the work than is normally the case. Whereas Scott, for example, adds chapter-mottoes less as an integral element or guide to meaning, than as a kind of decoration, and as a game between himself and his reader, MacDonald's mottoes can be extraordinarily helpful: because this rhetorically indirect work lacks his own commentating voice, they are the sole direct aid that he, as author, provides. Furthermore, they often seem to pinpoint the actual source in MacDonald's reading which gives rise to the contents of a chapter.

What books contain is the result of the activity, within authors, of Phantastes, and one's memories of books can be as precious as the memories of what Phantastes has prompted in one's own mind. Memory, indeed, is seen by MacDonald as the faculty which transforms the power of one's formative experiences into a permanent resource. Nor is it a neutral medium, but it adds beauty and power to what is remembered: 'Even the memories of past pain are beautiful; and past delights, though beheld only through clefts in the grey clouds of sorrow, are lovely as Fairy Land' (p. 73). The memory is, like a mirror or a still sea, one of the agents of reflection (there is an element of punning in MacDonald's use of the word) which he extols at several points: 'Why are all reflections lovelier than what we call the reality? — not so grand or so strong, it may be, but always lovelier? Fair as is the gliding sloop on the shining sea, the wavering, trembling, unresting sail below is fairer still... All mirrors are magic mirrors. The commonest room is a room in a poem when I turn to the glass... There must be a truth involved in it, though we may but in part lay hold of the meaning. Even the memories of past pain are beautiful...' (pp. 72–3). A memory is thus an enhancement of the reality it looks back on. Not only can Anodos salve his conscience on leaving the Beech Tree by thinking how comforting the memory of their encounter will be to her, but he himself, echoing the Wordsworth of 'Tintern Abbey', relishes the idea that his reading in the fairy palace has had long-term effect. His reading there has been one of the many deaths and resurrections in his life:

> From many a sultry noon till twilight, did I sit in that grand hall, buried and risen again in these old books. And I trust I have carried away in my soul some of the exhalations of their undying leaves. In after hours of deserved or needful sorrow, portions of what I read there have often come to me again, with an unexpected comforting; which was not fruitless, even though the comfort might seem in itself groundless and vain. (p. 108)

It is in this context that Anodos tries so assiduously to remember and record his experiences in Fairyland, at times apologising for the limitations of his memory, as when he attempts to reproduce the two stories he read in the palace library, or when he recalls the Wise Woman's singing of the Ballad of Sir Aglovaile, or when, having acquired his shadow, he 'can attempt no consecutive account of my wanderings and adventures' (p. 65), until he reaches the palace. Such comments serve two purposes. They are ways of communicating the inevitable gap, when an artistic vision is given a concrete embodiment, between the two: the attempt to catch the living inspiration is like the attempts of Anodos, in the palace, to burst in on the dancing figures behind the curtain by quelling his conscious intention and relying entirely on irrational impulse. Secondly, these comments are reminders that the whole work is a piece of recollection. *Phantastes* is the enactment of a mind trying to reach the bliss of which it has knowledge, and memory is the tool which that mind must use. Not only does Anodos have the recollection of his reading in the fairy palace, or his knowledge of how comforting the memory of the Wise Woman's promise can be, but he also has the example of how memory got him into Fairyland in the first place. The opening chapter is itself made up of the recollection of the strange events of the night before, and it seems to be the act of recollection which causes him to be translated to Fairyland: 'While these strange events were passing through my mind, I suddenly, as one awakes to the consciousness that the sea has been moaning by him for hours, or that the storm has been howling about his window all night, became aware of the sound of running water near me...' (p. 19). Thus, the whole book is a double attempt to achieve a wondrous translation into Fairyland — double in that it is both Anodos's and George MacDonald's. MacDonald's art, here and elsewhere, is an art of memory. At the outset of his career as a writer of fiction, he here creates an illustration of how he views art as a matter of reaching the goal of comfort and understanding through the creation of works based on the contents of his mind — based, that is, on his recollections of his life and his reading. Assiduous as they would remain throughout his career, *Phantastes* and old Eumnestes never served him, their noble Prince, better.

In a passage from a much later work, *The Diary of an Old Soul*, MacDonald, looking towards a time when writing will come hard to him, confirms how memory interacts with present utterance to the benefit, in the first instance, of himself:

> Not what I think, but what thou art, makes sure
> This utterance of spirit through still thought,
> This forming of heart-stuff in moulds of brain
> Is helpful to the soul by which 'tis wrought,
> The shape reacting on the heart again;
> But when I am quite old, and words are slow,
> Like dying things that keep their holes for woe,
> And memory's withering tendrils clasp with effort vain,
> Thou, then as now, no less wilt be my life...
>   (Old Soul, p. 137; 'October', 18,7 — 20,1)

How much of his writing, one wonders, was the creation of shapes which reacted again upon his heart?

In his last years, words ceased altogether, but in nearly his final effort of literary utterance he created in *Lilith* a work which gives no hint that the words had become any slower. Indeed, *Lilith* is conspicuous for the stylistic poise and tight verbal control for which it has no superior in his output. What *has* changed, to some extent, is the reliance on memory: the absence of chapter mottoes may be an outward sign of a different genesis from that of *Phantastes*, although, at first glance, it would appear that it is to the method of that youthful work that he had returned. In place of the comforting contemplation of the past, we find in the later fantasy an urgent message for a comfortless present. Greville MacDonald tells us that his father 'was possessed by a feeling' that *Lilith* 'was a mandate

direct from God, for which he himself was to find form
and clothing' (GMDW, p. 548). If God seems to be
intervening directly, there is perhaps less need to draw
on a purely human resource such as memory; certainly,
MacDonald embarked on a composition of remarkable
speed and freedom, swiftly creating the book's essential
symbols, 'over which he did not ponder' (GMDW, p.
548). It was as if the symbols were the mandate, and
the search for 'form and clothing' committed him to a
process somewhat unusual in his writing of fiction: the
work went through a long series of revisions so that
although it was embarked upon in 1890, it was not
published until 1895.[8] Hence the impression it gives of
combining arresting, living imagery with an unusual
control in style and structure.

It is obviously a much more highly wrought work
than *Phantastes*. While the basic narrative is
MacDonald's familiar one of the journey, it is far from
the predictably linear, picaresque sequence of the
earlier fantasy. Indeed, the convolutions of Vane's
interweavings between the worlds of three and seven
dimensions, and the complexity induced by apparent
retreats which turn out to be further stages of progress,
suggest what many critics have denied: MacDonald
does have a profound and sure sense of structure. The
aura of control, so marked in the total shape, is
repeated in details. For example, the riddles and
paradoxes which so frustrate Vane when Mr. Raven
utters them in the early stages of their relationship
reappear in Vane's mouth at the end, when, having
buried Lilith's hand, he is confronted by the
greyheaded man who longs to die (p. 395): the
structural echo, revealing just how far Vane has come,
is deft and telling.

One notes, too, that the wealth of interpolated poems
and narratives, so deliberately characteristic of *Phantastes*,
has been banished almost completely. When such things

do appear, as in 'My Father's Manuscript', and in the extracts from the poem with which Adam masters Lilith in Chapter Twenty-Nine, their purpose is clear and intimately entwined with the progress of the work. The complexity, and challenge to interpretation, of the book's symbols and incidents is acute enough for MacDonald to have no need to impose a narrative maze as he had delighted in doing in the earlier work. Echoes and parallelisms are the order of the day, rather, as when he works towards a unity by the repeated use of the motif of reflected sunlight. Regularly, through the book, crucial developments are initiated by the sudden reflection of beams of sunlight from a shiny surface on to an object to be highlighted — a picture, or a book in the library, or the mirror in the attic, or Lilith herself in the elliptical chamber of her brain.

Similarly, the verbal expression is clear, poised and controlled. McGillis has demonstrated how MacDonald worked towards greater simplicity and concentration in successive versions. Even without such scholarly information, however, the reader can appreciate the strange but effectively calculated combination of natural, simple clarity with elevated, enriching, faintly archaic structures and language, as in (at random) 'When I came to the precipice, I took my way betwixt the branches, for I would pass again by the cottage of Mara, lest she should have returned: I longed to see her once more ere I went to sleep; and now I knew where to cross the channels, even if the river should have overtaken me and filled them' (p. 394). This enriched style proves an entirely satisfactory medium for this tale, and appears to come to MacDonald with a natural inevitability echoing the naturalness of his lifelong heightened sense of reality.

Lilith, in fact, is designed less as an experience into which the reader must plunge, as *Phantastes* with its over-arching offer of imaginative delight pre-eminently is, than as a riddle which must be solved — like the universe described to Vane as he sets off on his journey through the strange land: 'The universe is a riddle trying to get out' (p. 226). The urgency of the message makes MacDonald strive to communicate where, in *Phantastes*, the reader's bewilderment was a conscious intention. MacDonald frequently indicates to his reader that if something is not understood, maturity will eventually bring understanding. Comprehension, both by Vane and the reader, seems much more immanent than it did in *Phantastes*. Meaning is obscured merely by the thin surface of appearances rather than by the deeper inconsequentiality of the earlier work, and so the indirections *Lilith* adopts are the transparent ones not only of allegory and symbol, but even those of satire, with an open freedom quite alien to *Phantastes*. In *Phantastes* the applicability to the reader of what is encountered in Fairyland is left delightfully compromised by its dream-status and by the stress (as we have seen) on Anodos's wondering exploration of his own memory, but in *Lilith* the reader is encouraged to believe in the reality of what is displayed. Vane presents his recollections firmly: though he again claims that his words are inadequate to embody his memories, the prevailing sureness of utterance leaves us little scope for doubting what he describes. Nor does Vane seem to be using memory to bring about wondrous benefits to himself, as Anodos does. The reader, rather, is Vane's concern. While it is true that, in reading of Anodos's experiences, we believe in the fairyland he traverses and remembers or imagines, the world into which Vane stumbles has an additional quality of *being there*. It has a firm, objective geography capable of being traversed many times: it has a physical independence which can be calculated upon, and entering or quitting it can be chosen and organised, to some extent. Indeed, at times

Vane's attitude to it is that of the Victorian explorer with a duty to bring back the secrets of dark continents. MacDonald is insisting on the inescapable tangibility of a region where eternal choices are made and conflicts fought out. He is insisting, too, on its proximity to, and inter-relatedness with, the familiar world. Therefore its machinery of Wellsian science-fiction replaces the age-old dream-convention which served well enough in *Phantastes*: the pseudo-science of reflected polarised light provides a link between the two worlds which seems more difficult to gainsay.

The world of *Lilith*, furthermore, is a much more terrifying place than that of its predecessor, where horrors such as the Alder-maiden and the Ash are fairly rare. Vane's first encounters with the very fact of another world induce in him fears which have no counterpart in Anodos and, once properly into it, he finds it full of utterly horrific experiences. Where the opening of *Phantastes* is in a fairytale mode, the manner of *Lilith's* opening is that of the ghost-story. Poe is sometimes mentioned, rightly, as a comparison and as a possible influence, but the intensity of such scenes as that in which Vane is attacked by Mara's cats (pp. 333–34), or the arrival of Vane in Bulika (pp. 298–300) — let alone the power of Lilith's final scenes with Mara and Adam — negate any suspicions that MacDonald's solemn gothic power is essentially second-hand. Much of the book's imagery derives from a charnel vein which MacDonald always loved but which in this book about death receives its full justification. It was this quality of imagery which so upset MacDonald's wife (GMDW, p. 548). If MacDonald risks overdoing the imagery of nightmare, so that the novel seems to shriek at times, it is a sign of his urge to create a clear and forceful message about the reality of evil and the nature of death.

In line with this urge to vehement clarity is the

explicit religiousness of some of the imagery and references. In his discussion of 'The *Lilith* Manuscripts', Roderick McGillis is pleased to report that, in successive versions, MacDonald deletes more and more direct references to God with a view to broadening the interest of the work beyond the theological and dealing, instead, with states of being.[9] While it is true that *Lilith* is far less explicit about its religious allegiances than the novels are, it is still far more openly Christian in its colouring than *Phantastes*, and unequivocal enough by any standards in its references to 'the perfect meal' of bread and wine (p. 211), to Adam and Eve, to resurrection and to heaven and hell. It keeps its distance from God, who is mentioned only rarely, but this is because the point of view is that of the groping Vane who at best is allowed only fleeting proximity to the throne of the Ancient of Days. MacDonald is reserved about referring to God, not because he wants to be understood in a sense wider than the religious (I doubt if he could imagine a wider sense than that) but because he had that sturdy Calvinist belief in the distance between God and man — and between God and man's imagination. The novels can refer frequently and intimately to God because their clear confinement to our own fallen world retains the sense of the great gulf. In fantasy works, however, the barrier is down and the creation of worlds where higher and deeper truths are visible might give the appearance of a claim to insight which the author would never wish to make. Restraint, indirection, and the drawing of parallels are the necessary methods of a Calvin-formed fantasist like MacDonald; indeed, what is remarkable about *Lilith* in this respect is how explicit it is.

Both the early and late fantasies succeed in suggesting that man is embedded in a much vaster and more mysterious system of truth than he normally realises, but the universe in *Lilith* has the firmer, more schematic structure: Vane has to fit in to it and discover its secrets, where Anodos wandered through a landscape which was more completely orientated towards him. In *Lilith*, more is at stake than Vane's inner growth: his behaviour brings responsibilities beyond his own improvement and his actions can be decisive in aiding or retarding the spread of evil as a whole. Hence, in part, the greater urgency and seriousness which marks the later work. That moral urgency, too, seems instrumental in greatly reducing the importance of art in the book's scale of values, when compared with *Phantastes*. The theme has lost most of its earlier prominence, though it can still be discerned at moments such as Vane's first stumbling through the mirror — he first views the scene in the frame as a painting and leans forward, connoisseur-like, 'to examine the texture of a stone in the immediate foreground' (p. 193). This minimal moment of self-forgetful awareness tips him into the other world. More generally, his bookishness seems to be a rudimentary factor in rendering him a candidate for other-worldly adventures, as the centrality of the library in the early action indicates. Other hints of a lingering concern with art may be found in the scene with the skull-headed dancers, whose dance 'vaguely embodied the story of life, its meetings, its passions, its partings' (p. 263). This seems a rather earth-bound set of implications, however, far from the other-worldly communications that art sometimes achieved in *Phantastes*.

What is *Lilith* about? Greville tells us that his father wrote it as a warning against 'the increasingly easy tendencies of universalists, who, because they had now discarded everlasting retribution as a popular superstition, were dismissing hell-fire altogether, and with it the need for repentance as the way back into the Kingdom. With hell incarnate in ugliness and falsehood all about and within, we are prone to find comfort in declaring that Evil is but shadow cast by the Light, the devil but an imagined symbol of the distress caused by darkness; and to find Hell a tolerably comfortable caravanserai' (GMDW, pp. 551–52). As we have seen, evil, in this book, is no longer naturally overcome by the mere onward flow of events: the narrative twists back on itself and lays the onus for a happy outcome much more firmly on the moral choices of the hero. In comparison, too, with the evil creatures of *Phantastes*, Lilith herself is much more of an independent and tangible character — she is no mere shadow of the hero's psyche. Furthermore, the Shadow of this book is more than absence of light but, rather, a tangible blackness, as little Odu describes after the Shadow passes through him (p. 360). More fundamentally still, the state that finally induces Lilith to acquiesce in Mara's demands for submission is worse than the absence of God. MacDonald strives to suggest that that ultimate absence is, more menacingly, a fearful presence so awful as to terrify Lilith into submission as well as to be tangible to an onlooker like Vane: 'A horrible Nothingness, a Negation positive infolded her; the border of its being that was yet no being, touched me, and for one ghastly instant I seemed alone with Death Absolute! It was not the absence of everything I felt, but the presence of Nothing' (p. 375). In such a passage, MacDonald risks even the impression of Manicheism in his urgent attempt to insist on the reality and danger of evil.

Not that MacDonald has reverted to a simple belief in the Calvinist scheme of things: he has the harder task (harder than merely accepting or rejecting the notion of the fiery pit) of redefining hell as a state which, while terrible, is part of a benign scheme — a state which actually induces the self-knowledge and revulsion which propels erring creatures into accepting the will of God. A clear-cut example is the skeleton lord and lady who, comically, continue their earthly bickering and folly until they begin, out of sheer necessity, to build a better relationship with each other. Beholding them, Mr. Raven is quite explicit that hell is a state, not a place: 'You are not in hell. Neither am I in hell. But those skeletons are in hell!' (p. 271). So, undoubtedly, is Lilith as she is subjected, by Mara, to the torture of self-knowledge. As this phase begins, Vane is aware that 'a soundless presence as of roaring flame possessed the house' and Lilith burns 'in the hell of her self-consciousness' (pp. 372; 373).

If a large part of *Lilith* is the redefinition and vivification of the notion of hell, an even larger part of the book's purpose is to do the same for death. As ever, MacDonald intimately links the idea with that of a break-through into selflessness, thus preaching two hard lessons at once: overcoming one's selfishness is as hard and as fundamental as dying while, conversely, dying is simply the stage at which one becomes a better person. The moral climax of *Phantastes* is reached when Anodos sacrifices himself for the sake of others by destroying the evil ceremony, thereby liberating himself to a state of blissful love and service to others. He has become a resurrected primrose, to be gathered to the bosom of his lady. Vane's corresponding death lacks all the attractive trappings of chivalrous action: he must coldly, consciously lie down in the grave, and the imagery of plant-life is transmuted from Anodos's primrose-resurrection to the bulb itself dormant in the frozen earth. This serves to underline the physical burial ('I lay at peace, full of the quietest expectation, breathing the damp odours of Earth's bountiful bosom') and forces on the reader the paradox that the traditional horrors of the grave ('How cold I was, words cannot tell...') are themselves the transition-point between woe and bliss ('...yet I grew colder and colder — and welcomed the cold yet more and more'.)

For 'I grew continuously less conscious of myself, continuously more conscious of bliss, unimaginable yet felt' (p. 400).

In the geography of the other world, Adam's cottage, with its vast graveyard containing Vane's allotted resting-place, lies nearest, of all the other-worldly locations, to Vane's house: the challenge of, and opportunity for, death (especially in its sense of dying to oneself) is the first of the higher realities to be encountered. At first, of course, Vane cannot do so and flees in horror from the graveyard. When he returns soon after, however, having changed his mind, he is judged to be not ready for death, after all, and instead must undergo the various adventures which make up the main body of the narrative. Right knowledge of death is the book's ultimate goal. When Vane first flees from the nocturnal hospitality of Mr. and Mrs. Raven, he does not fully know what it is that he is rejecting, so that his contrary impulse, after having read his father's manuscript, to take up their offer is equally ill-founded. Full, accepting knowledge is needed, in MacDonald's view, before one can fully die, for only thus can the self be destroyed. It is to gain this knowledge that Mr. Raven sends him off on his journey, having denied him a place among the dead for the moment. Vane gains that knowledge primarily by encountering two embodiments of inadequate knowledge of death, Lilith and the Little Ones, and by watching their correction.

Lilith is not merely an embodiment of evil: more crucially, she is the incarnation of the belief that death is a horror — hence her rebellion against God and Adam. The poem with which Adam penetrates through to her undisguised self in Chapter Twenty-nine is a versification of her (and our) revulsion against the physical corruption of the grave: her belief that that is all that physical death amounts to is also allowed to stand as a symbol for her concept of the loss of self.

Lilith's evil is seen as rooted in an obsession with the corruption of the flesh which utterly perverts what is divine in her nature.

An overriding result of that perversion is the utter negation of maternal feeling in her, and her consequent hatred of the Little Ones, especially her own daughter, Lona. The colony of the Little Ones clearly represents innocent goodness, but they, too, are in a state of unhealthy ignorance of the truth of death, because they are as ignorant of the end of earthly life as they are of its beginnings. They do not fear death, therefore, as Lilith does, but they are aware of, and fear, one who is closely related to Adam and his world of death, namely Mara, whose name signifies bitterness (see Ruth, 1, 20). Their fear of the cat-woman Mara is an allegory of the human instinct to shun pain and sorrow, and it is a fear they must overcome if they, too, are to die — as they, like all things created, must. MacDonald's final urgent message to the world is to teach us to die.

As he sets off on the journey which will involve him with Lilith and the Little Ones, Vane is provided by Mr. Raven with a rainbow-coloured 'bird-butterfly' — one of those symbols, like the air-fish in 'The Golden Key' and the rainbow imagery of *Alec Forbes*, by which MacDonald suggests the transitory goals which draw us into and through experience. After stumbling after it for a little way, however, Vane grasps at the gorgeous light, only to find that 'a dead book with boards outspread lay cold and heavy in my hand' (p. 228). Critics such as Wolff and Hein have been hard on Vane at this point, believing that the episode embodies the dire effects of supplanting unthinking delight with the grasping rationalism of the human intellect.[10] Yet in this of all books, images of death, cold and 'boards outspread' are not elsewhere deplored — nor are books otherwise objects of scorn. The creature, gorgeous as it appeared, was hardly a suitable guide for Vane (any more than Mr. Raven's riddles convey information to him): attempting to follow it, he keeps stumbling and once knocks himself out. Furthermore, it is happy to give itself to Vane, for it sinks towards him. It may be that Vane's fault is in rejecting 'the treasure of the universe' in the bookish form which he is capable of grasping and benefiting from. The despised rationality of its contents might have saved him from the terrors which he now endures as he crosses the Bad Burrow, where the monsters, we learn near the end of the book, symbolise the unhealthy thoughts of which the human mind is capable (see p. 413). At any rate, the creature, evanescent and temporary like all MacDonald's rainbow-guides, has served its purpose in pointing out an initial direction.

There is clearly scope for some disagreement and confusion in the interpretation of this little episode. (Not even those who accuse Vane of culpable, rationalistic grasping eschew a rational, allegorical reading of the incident.) It is a confusion, moreover, symptomatic of the heart of a work which, despite all its excellence, seems unclear as to how Vane and his actions are to be assessed. During the argument later in the book, when Vane succumbs to the temptation to ride to the aid of the Little Ones without first sleeping in the House of the Dead, Adam proclaims that 'nearly the only foolish thing you ever did, was to run from our dead' (p. 331), an assessment at variance with his earlier view that 'your night was not come then, or you would not have left us' (p. 224). In the same argument, Adam is dogmatic, with all the weight of the book's apparent authority behind him, that Vane can achieve nothing without first sleeping the sleep of death. Vane disobeys, however, and certainly runs into a catalogue of perils, disappointments and disasters, culminating in the death of Lona. Nevertheless, the prophecy concerning the downfall of Lilith is achieved, the Little

Ones are rescued from their unknowing innocence, and Vane is at last endowed with enough knowledge of the rights and wrongs of the universe for him to accept death. Despite Adam's alternative advice, Vane appears to have done the right thing.

When Vane and Adam next meet, Lilith having been released into the sleep of death, the hero's disobedience and its consequences are slurred over in two brief sentences ('Is he forgiven, husband?' 'From my heart'. — p. 391). It was open to MacDonald to make a point about good being brought about from evil had he wanted to. That he does not would suggest that his heart is with the broad implication of the narrative, that Vane, with all his imperfection, is the necessary agent for the eventual triumph of good. The conflict goes deeper than this one book, for it is really a reflection of how MacDonald's creed of the virtue of action essentially conflicts with his belief that God is all in all and human effort, considered as a thing itself, vain. The key moment is Vane's disobedience. Adam urges him, above all things, to wait and sleep, causing Vane to exclaim 'But surely sleep is not the first thing! Surely, surely, action takes precedence of repose!' (p. 328). These are not questions, as we might have expected, but (with the reiterated 'surely') cries from the heart, and they seem to come ultimately from the heart of the creator of such athletically active heroes as Malcolm, Gibbie and the young Alec Forbes. All MacDonald's instincts were towards the active assault upon evil, but he also realised that in even the most righteous fights there is some self-glorification. The lesson of *Lilith* seems to be that righteous action should not be undertaken until the self is utterly dead, but such an impossible condition was of no use to an author who was, in his son's words, 'always a fighter'.[11]

If MacDonald cannot wait to finally obliterate self in order to render righteous action pure and possible, nor can he finally imagine death, though the closing chapters of his book seem to commit him to doing so. It is not simply that, not having physically died, he does not know what it is like. More fundamentally still, death cannot even be imagined in its ultimate fullness because to do so would require the complete abandonment of any last sense of the self. As MacDonald understands it, death is the utter abandonment of self — the complete negation of identity. (Such, too, is William Golding's conception in *Pincher Martin*, where the imagined survival after physical death is the result of Pincher's ferocious selfishness.) The final obliteration of self is not in the scope of the creature — any more than the completion of the final needful act, the opening of her hand, is within Lilith's power, so God's representative, Adam, cuts it off instead. For Vane, the equivalent of that blow from Adam's sword would be to have been admitted into the 'deep folds' of God's cloudy skirts, disappearing irrevocably into a region beyond the scope of human imagination.

The ending is designed to enact the supreme state of possible human detachment from the everyday world, and to convey the limitations of that state, for the final chapter is shot through with tension, doubt and sadness. The denial of self means total reliance on God, even for the contents of one's thoughts and dreams. Even when doubt is challenged, it is not by Vane himself, but by Hope personified. Yet, having foresworn all the activity which defines and creates our world in our perception, Vane finds that world itself becoming insubstantial and dreamlike, an awareness which maintains the steady pressure of doubt on the fringes of his consciousness. Vane is caught between Self and God, between ignorance and knowledge, between frustration and contentment. Hence the tension in the bald final statement of what he knows: 'I wait; asleep or awake, I wait'. He stresses the little he is sure of —

his waiting — and the repetition enacts his commitment to the self-thwarting which is killing his self, but he cannot restrain the self, with its doubt, ignorance, and weariness, from momentarily swelling out with the alternatives which plague him. The sentence suggests a man grimly and wearily adhering to the abandonment of earthly life. We sense his momentary relief as he escapes into the hopeful words of another — Novalis — in the final sentence.

NOTES

1. Giles and Phineas Fletcher, *Poetical Works* (2 vols.), ed. F. S. Boas, Cambridge, 1909, II, 79.
2. All references are to the edition of *Phantastes* and *Lilith* first published by Gollancz in 1962 and reprinted several times.
3. *The Poems of Matthew Arnold*, ed. Kenneth Allott, 2nd edition, ed. M. Allott, London and New York, 1979, p. 253.
4. C. N. Manlove, *The Impulse of Fantasy Literature*, London, 1983, p. 92; Rolland Hein, *The Harmony Within: The Spiritual Vision of George MacDonald*, Grand Rapids, 1982, pp. 54–84; David Holbrook, 'Introduction' to *Phantastes*, London, Melbourne & Toronto, 1983, pp. vii–xxv.
5. C. S. Lewis, *George MacDonald: An Anthology*, London, 1946, p. 14.
6. Lewis, p. 16.
7. Hein, p. 55.
8. Roderick F. MacGillis, 'George MacDonald — The *Lilith* Manuscripts' in *Scottish Literary Journal*, 4, 2, December 1977, pp. 40–57.
9. MacGillis, p. 56.
10. R. L. Wolff, *The Golden Key: A Study of the Fiction of George MacDonald*, New Haven, 1961, pp. 340–41; Hein, p. 91.
11. Greville MacDonald, *Reminiscences of a Specialist*, London, 1932, p. 322.

CHAPTER 5

FICTION FOR THE CHILD

Taking the place of the traditional devil-figure, Lilith is a cunning deployment, by MacDonald, of a character whom he can portray as reclaimable by heaven. Had he used the familiar Satan, and tried to tell the same story of an ultimate change of heart — an ultimate salvation — it would have been distractingly and needlessly controversial. Furthermore, a female symbol was needed to make more effective the particular interpretation of evil MacDonald wished to make in his final major book: Lilith's over-riding impulse, once pride has induced her to rebel against God and Adam, is to destroy both her child Lona and also childlikeness, as embodied in the Little Ones, in general. It is as if MacDonald were envisaging the battle between Good and Evil — the Battle of Armageddon, as he discusses it in *Malcolm* — as meaning the conflict between the childlike vision and the adult, or parental, viewpoint. If this seems, at first sight, a somewhat eccentric and limiting interpretation of the great universal conflict, a glance at the opening sermon in the first of MacDonald's three volumes of *Unspoken Sermons* can help.[1] It is entitled 'The Child in the Midst': childhood is MacDonald's starting-point in his main explicit exposition of his Christian belief. There he states, swiftly and categorically, the 'the *childlike* is the divine' (US, p. 3) and reminds his readers how Jesus told the disciples that 'they could not enter into the kingdom save by becoming little children — by humbling themselves' (US, p. 8). Childlikeness is opposed, in his mind, to pride (the root of Satan's, and Lilith's, fall) so that a refusal to adopt the child's vision is to repeat that initial fault. And he goes further.

> He who receives a child, then, in the name of Jesus, does so, perceiving wherein Jesus and the child are one, what is common to them. He must not only see the *ideal* child in the child he receives — that reality of loveliness which constitutes true childhood, but must perceive that the child is like Jesus, or rather, that the Lord is like the child, and may be embraced, yea, is embraced, by every heart childlike enough to embrace a child for the sake of his childness. (US, pp. 11–12)

Not only is every child like Christ, but to cherish, or even to recognise, the childlike, is to become like Christ oneself. With this startingly direct equation between the child and Christ in mind, therefore, we can make much more sense of Lilith's behaviour: in her enmity to the Little Ones, she is opposing herself to the Good at the heart of the universe. In fact, the Little Ones are only the last of many instances in MacDonald's fiction in which childhood is presented as being a particular point of attack by evil (Annie Anderson persecuted by Malison and the Bruces in *Alec Forbes*, Phemy Mair kidnapped by the evil howdie in *Malcolm*, young Sir Gibbie fleeing from murder and whipped till insensibility, etc). In addition, the equation helps explain the peculiar power and authority with which MacDonald invests certain of his young characters: for example, Alec Forbes himself (who embodies the 'spirit of loons' which is locked in combat with Robert Bruce's selfish materialism), the infant Old Man of the Fire in 'The Golden Key' and the holy fool Gibbie Galbraith.

It seems appropriate, perhaps even predictable, that a writer who gave the child such a central place in his ideology should have been the author of works now counted among the classics of Victorian fiction for children. Indeed, there is a seeming inevitability about the fact that it is MacDonald's children's books which have achieved the most sustained popularity — and availability in print — of all his writings. Clearly, his veneration for the child gave him more than a measure of sympathy with children, and the ability to address them effectively. Just as clearly, it was in this mode that his particular tastes and talents found the readiest acceptability: the fantasy-world of the fairy-tale was a ready-made medium for the imaginative freedom he so often needed. Writing for children, it would have been hard for him to do what he does so often elsewhere — namely to baffle and annoy sophisticated readers with the various denials of probability which most of his work evinces.

His children's fiction, therefore, seems to constitute a separate and especially successful category within his output. Yet its separateness from the rest of his work can be exaggerated and, indeed, the more one considers the matter the more integrated into the corpus of his writing it seems. The same characters-types, plot situations, images and symbols, apparently from a stock pool, occur throughout the body of his work. The dividing-line between the so-called 'adult' fantasies and the writing for children is obviously narrow, if it really exists at all, but, more surprisingly, the gap between the 'realistic novels' and the writing for children is also much narrower than we might have expected. Among the Scottish novels (the 'realistic' novels with which this book has been concerned), several (particularly *Alec Forbes* and *Robert Falconer*) have a major proportion of their lengths given over to the childhoods of their heroes and heroines, and are clearly close to the world of, say, *Ranald Bannerman's Boyhood*, a novel for children which is discussed later in this chapter. Others, again, deal in whole or in large part with adolescent adventures (the above, plus, for example, *Malcolm*, *Donal Grant* and *Castle Warlock*). The genre of the adventure story for boys is palpably close in much of MacDonald's adult writing, and so is the world of fairytale, as I have argued earlier (see above, p. 49). Despite obvious but superficial differences of mode, all MacDonald's fiction patently comes from the same imagination and, its peculiar success notwithstanding, the writing for children is really no different.

Obviously, one cannot simply argue that there is nothing about the children's fiction which marks it out as 'for children'. The imaginative surfaces of these works are meant to appeal to the young, and can still do so: the fantasies about good and bad fairies and goblins, or many of the adventures of Ranald Bannerman, have a natural juvenile appeal. Just as important, MacDonald's consciousness of his young audience leads him (usually) to a more simple and direct style which can be more limpidly refreshing than much of his adult writing. Yet the over-riding feature which, at face value, seems to locate these works as for children — the fact that child characters are utterly central to them — is of little help in differentiating them from much else that MacDonald wrote. Furthermore, MacDonald can occasionally be seen forgetting that it is children he is supposed to be addressing as he lapses into discussions for adult readers, nowhere so obviously as at the end of Chapter 20 of *Ranald Bannerman's Boyhood*. ('But I find I have been forgetting that those for whom I write are young — too young to understand this. Let it remain, however...') Here and often elsewhere, he cannot resist making points which seem to him to be true and important, however inappropriate they may be to his junior readers. Such moments occur sufficiently frequently for one to doubt whether his writing is being completely and securely controlled by a sense of the tender years of his audience. The task of writing specifically for children is less fundamental to him than the impulse to write as truly as he can — which is the goal he always sets himself elsewhere. His junior audiences often have to take him as they find him, just as his adult readers must.

This might appear to be a way of saying that his writing for children is also writing for adults, and we may be tempted to suspect that here we have the secret of his status as a classic children's author: such works as *Alice in Wonderland* and *Treasure Island* appear to have their stature depend, in part at least, on the esteem and interest of adults. Is there any great children's book which seems great because children, alone, have so designated it? C. S. Lewis said that 'I am almost inclined to set it up as a canon that a children's story which is enjoyed only by children is a bad children's story'.[2] In addition, the complex question of what makes for great children's literature is complicated by that occasional process whereby books written with a purely adult audience in view are relegated (the usual word) to the nursery to become children's classics. As Jacqueline Rose has recently pointed out, even *Peter Pan* was created for adult audiences.[3]

In MacDonald's case, we have an author who is constantly preoccupied with the largest issues, so it can seem inevitable that his children's writing is not just for children. Yet, as we have seen, his adult writing is not just for adults — it is for the child in each of them. Who, then, is MacDonald writing for? In an important sense, he is writing for himself. The discussion Ronald MacDonald reports (see above, p. 21) can be taken to indicate not merely his father's profound sense of duty but also his inability to redirect his writing away from his own preoccupations and out towards the tastes and preferences of a readership. Not only do his works ceaselessly explore and articulate his own, very personal set of beliefs and priorities but, as we have frequently seen, they draw to an immense extent on his own memories and fantasies. To a considerable extent, MacDonald writes to explore and confirm, to himself, the meaning and significance of his own life, beliefs and recollections. *Phantastes*, his first major work of fiction, illustrates the process time and time again.

And it is in his writing for children, where his sense of a clear audience other than himself appears to be firmest, that we find him, I believe, at his most inward. For if the themes of his principal pieces of children's fiction are examined, we find that they are focused on insights or topics particularly liable to trouble the mind. Ever since his own lifetime, MacDonald has been regarded as offering a particularly optimistic message. Occasionally, in Greville's biography, we are allowed to glimpse his father's moments of doubt or difficulty and, strangely, it is in the writing for children that we find worries being confronted most directly. To illustrate this, let us look at his best work in this vein, and concentrate on the books he wrote for *Good Words for the Young* (Nov. 1868 — Oct. 1872), the editorship of which he took over from Norman Macleod for the second, third and final volumes. Here appeared, among other MacDonald contributions, *At the Back of the North Wind*, *Ranald Bannerman's Boyhood* and *The Princess and the Goblin*.

This last, however, had a sequel, *The Princess and Curdie* which was published as a book in 1882 and so lies outside the *Good Words* period. Nevertheless, it is not only a strong work in itself, but provides the most immediately clear evidence of the point I am making. It is among MacDonald's most sustained and deeply-felt comments on the materialism of his age, which is one of his many constant themes. No other work of his, however, matches this for the sustained focus on the topic, or for the grimness of his mood as he handles it. It is a book which clearly worries many of

MacDonald's admirers, who are especially disturbed by
its aggressively pessimistic ending. MacDonald grants
the stock fairytale ending to his princess and miner's
son, with their marriage and happy rule over the city of
Gwyntystorm, but this is perfunctorily done and he
unexpectedly looks forward to the later history of the
place after they have gone. Greedy mining for gold
undermines the foundations:

> One day at noon, when life was at its highest, the
> whole city fell with a roaring crash. The cries of
> men and the shrieks of women went up with its
> dust, and then there was a great silence.
>
> Where the mighty rock once towered, crowded
> with homes and crowned with a palace, now
> rushes and raves a stone-obstructed rapid of the
> river. All around spreads a wilderness of wild deer,
> and the very name of Gwyntystorm had ceased
> from the lips of men. (P&C, p. 221)

Marion Lochhead takes this as signalling a severe
crisis in MacDonald, and indicating a complete,
temporary loss of faith and optimism.[4] Wolff sees this
conclusion as an expression of the utmost pessimism,
for evil has triumphed and even the powerful
grandmother–goddess provides no salvation. He writes
of MacDonald as being like 'a man in despair, not
resigned, but angry with an anger he felt to be futile'.[5]
He rightly relates the ending, however, to the rest of
the book which, all through, is an angry and trenchant
comment (indeed, a satire) on Victorian Britain. (Note
how eager MacDonald is to tell his reader about the
failings of Gwyntystorm when Curdie approaches it,
and to denounce the overweening complacency and
unfounded sense of superiority of his own age. Later, in
outlining the response of the citizenry to the recovery of
the king and the expulsion of the wicked servants from
the palace, he takes time to lay bare the philosophy of

the place in his account of the sermon on the theme of selfishness, with text taken from *The Book of Nations* — presumably a comment on his age's devotion to the creed summed up by Adam Smith.)

It is true that not only one's experience of MacDonald's habit of happy endings but, more powerfully, one's expectation that the fairytale convention will be undisturbed, makes this outcome very surprising. Yet it is in accord with the book as a whole, which has convincingly portrayed Curdie's triumph over the evils of Gwyntystorm as hard, precarious and protracted, requiring the utmost force (down to the physical maiming of the worst offenders). Instead of registering dismay at MacDonald's pessimism or reproving the author for the severity of the punishments he imagines, it is surely primarily incumbent on the critic to welcome a work of particular power and artistic coherence.

MacDonald's preoccupation with the corrosive destructiveness of materialism, and with the precariousness of the combat of good and evil, can be felt in the opening pages where he describes what mountains are. Nature is glorious in itself, and a sign of further glory, yet when its buried wealth is gathered the results can be either good or bad (hoarded, Nature's wealth 'grew diseased and was called *mammon*' — P&C, p. 12), and the miners who burrow are ambivalently viewed as understandably exploring marvellous regions for glorious treasure yet also as behaving destructively and childishly. Curdie, too, is portrayed in a more complex way than in the previous book. Where before he had been a simple incarnation of dauntless youthfulness, here he is shown as first developing in a commonplace, material-minded way. From this decline he is rescued by an Ancient Mariner-like passage of destruction (he shoots a dove with his bow) followed by self-revulsion and a saving encounter with the old princess in the tower.

A particular purpose in his cleansing is that he be endowed with the magic ability to tell, on holding the hand of another, what animal-nature lurks in the person he confronts, and most of those Curdie encounters are hypocrites whose moral state is progressing downwards through the animal kingdom. In this book, above all, men are seen as unstable — either improving or deteriorating, and the same can be said for their powers of effective moral action. Thus the king, who had seemed so all-powerful and masterful in *The Princess and the Goblin*, is here, for much of the book, held powerlessly in thrall by the machinations of disloyal servants until Curdie nurses him back to health. MacDonald's vision here, in other words, is not one of simple pessimism but of realistic recognition of the moral tensions and instabilities of human life. It is a return to the lesson taught a few years earlier by Malcolm's mentor, Alexander Graham, when he instructs a pupil that a man may be both good and bad, a situation of which he says 'That's the battle of Armageddon, Sheltie, my man. It's aye ragin', ohn gun roared or bagonet clashed. Ye maun up an' do yer best in't, my man' (M, p. 33; chap. 7, 'Alexander Graham'). Despite the ultimate glory of Malcolm's rule from Lossie House, there is no suggestion that the Battle of Armaggedon has been finally won. A victory such as Malcolm's — or Curdie's — is only a temporary respite. (The comparison of the *Princess* books with the Portlossie novels is not exhausted by these few remarks. Indeed, a close relationship can be seen throughout the two pairs of books, so that, to some degree, they are two different tellings of the same tale.)

This is not to argue away the startling effect of the end, nor to underestimate the depth of MacDonald's seriousness. Indeed, his deep seriousness here is exactly the point. Though we need not, I think, assume with Marion Lochhead a clear phase of mental darkness (comparable to the tradition of Shakespeare's supposed gloomy patch while writing *King Lear*), MacDonald certainly does give expression here to the anxiety which he, along with a very large number of Victorian thinkers, writers and churchmen, felt over a long period as regards the outlook of the age. Despite our knowledge of the sorrows of his family life in the period preceding the writing of the book, it still seems surprising that he should have articulated such a vision in a book allegedly for children.

The wonder seems compounded when we turn to the earlier works for children and find that they, too, are as revealing of some of MacDonald's innermost concerns — concerns which, at times, must have amounted to anxieties. *The Princess and the Goblin*, for example, is about belief itself, and about fear. The hierarchy of mines, castle and tower-room, with the princess located between the goblins below and her mysterious grandmother above, can tempt to a reading of Freudian allegory.[6] It seems better, however, to respond more directly to the tale, and to see the two regions between which Irene and Curdie are sandwiched as dimensions of reality of which we are normally unaware in our daily business. Grandmother inhabits a region of spiritual truth and safety, while the goblin caves represent the dangers of materialism.

Grandmother is clearly an embodiment of the divine principle; indeed, she might best be regarded as representing the divine in each of us. More immediately, she can be seen as a dimension of Princess Irene, for she shares her name and tells her 'I've been here ever since you came yourself' (P&G, p. 22). An important part of her function is to provide Irene with a place which feels like a home, and to be a source of guidance and safety — her gift of the miraculous guiding ball of thread is the most obvious instance of this. (Prior to this, Curdie has devised his own mundane clew: the need for guidance through the twists, turns and bafflements of life has, as I have suggested, a particular urgency in MacDonald's outlook.) In the scene in which she gives this gift, Irene says 'I'm so glad, grandmother, you didn't say "go home" for this is my home. Mayn't I call this my home?' (P&G, p. 108), thereby making us aware of something which we had realised only subconsciously prior to this: Irene's contentment has obscured the fact that her existence has been strangely lacking a proper domestic environment. She has accepted, without question, her separation from her parents, and she is not even properly informed when her mother dies. Irene embodies our habitual blindness to our own lack, and need, in being cut off from God. Yet when she is brought into contact with the God-like, in the person of her grandmother, she is instantly drawn to her, and her realisation that grandmother's domain is her real home is bound up with her possession of the magic thread.

Yet despite Irene's openness to her grandmother's influence, even she, the most accessible to divine perceptions of all the book's characters, finds that belief in the wonderful being above can be hard. After her second visit to the attic, when her grandmother had cured her hurt finger, Irene is put to the test of belief in her. Can her faith lead her to return at the predetermined interval of a week (the test resembles some of the trials of mesmeric power which William Gregory describes in his account of animal magnetism — see above, p. 15), or will a more commonplace interpretation prevail in Irene's mind so that she thinks her grandmother but a dream? The latter temptation is a real one, vividly and convincingly put before us, but it takes a fright from one of the goblin's creatures to drive her away, at the crucial moment, from the stair which leads to her grandmother. Later, when bolder action still is required of her, and she must follow her magic thread, wherever it may lead, to rescue the entombed Curdie, she does so in perfect security of faith. Indeed, for MacDonald, a central part of the meaning of being a princess (as ever, the outer social meaning is less important to him than the inner, symbolic one) is that princesses have precisely Irene's insight and faith.

It is against Irene's capacity for insight and belief that others are to be compared. Lootie, her nurse, is placed alongside her to embody how limiting spiritual blindness is, even in an essentially good-hearted and loving person. Lootie's stupidity is needed as a counterweight to the knowledge of the grandmother in the attic that the reader shares in accompanying Irene, so that the much more important difficulties of insight and belief experienced by Curdie arouse our sympathy and tolerance rather than our exasperation.

Curdie's inability to see Irene's grandmother when Irene leads him up to the attic is a master-stroke, causing the reader as much wonder and surprise as it causes Irene. But where the reader is allowed to feel some impatience with Lootie's dismissal of what Irene tells her, here he is allowed to appreciate to the full the difficulty Curdie faces and the consequent predicament the two children experience in the sudden disjunction of their vision. On Irene's part, Curdie's blindness is painful because she had hoped to prove the extraordinary tale behind her ability to lead him out of the mine. It is, to her, a moment of astonishment and intense disappointment when, in the presence of the truth which explains and clinches her ability, that self-evident truth is rejected. If a major theme of this work is the question of belief and its difficulty, an intimately-related facet is the anguish of knowing the truth and not being believed. MacDonald is writing out of the poignant experiences of the believer in an unbelieving world.

But, simultaneously, he is writing out of the knowledge of how hard, and at times impossible, belief is. Curdie's answer to the question as to what he sees in the attic is honest, detailed and even sensitive: in the 'big, bare, garret-room' he sees 'a tub, and a heap of musty straw, and a withered apple, and a ray of sunlight coming through a hole in the middle of the roof, and shining on your head, and making all the place look a curious dusky brown' (P&G, pp. 154–55). These poetic words, which MacDonald repeats almost exactly when he looks back on this moment in *The Princess and Curdie* several years later, convey Curdie's goodness and sensitivity as well as they convey his blindness, and MacDonald stresses the respect which is due to such an honestly limited vision when he makes Irene realise 'that for her not to believe him was at least as bad as for him not to believe her' (P&G, p. 154). Nor is it simply a matter of Curdie, with his earthly vision, being tolerated till he learns better. If *he* cannot see, in the aery attic regions, what Irene can see, *she*, conversely, had needed him to point out to her dangers in the depths of the mine, when they had to creep by in close proximity to the king and queen of the goblins: 'Irene shuddered when she saw the frightful creatures, whom she had passed without observing them' (P&G, p. 146). Throughout the book, Curdie's massive competence in dealing with the goblins makes him far more than simply a candidate for visionary education: he is an equal force, along with Irene, for effective good. In Curdie, MacDonald makes the case for the necessity and value of the virtuous man who is not, in the Scots phrase, far ben with God.

Nor is the difficulty of beholding the divine, or of believing in what one has not seen, the only troublesome issue which MacDonald handles in this work. The one instance when Irene is in some real danger of being separated from her great-grandmother

occurs when she is frightened and, in panic, she runs
out on to the hillside. This is one of many moments
when fear, experienced or threatening, is a major
concern. In part, MacDonald is simply concerned to
confront the ever-present spirit of anxiety which was
one of the leading characteristics of the age.[7] More
narrowly, this tale of a spiritually sensitive princess
threatened by goblins from the mines is an allegory of
the fears which can beset believers in their religious
lives. It is not just that fear is a painful emotion, to be
avoided for its unpleasantness and because it disables
one's everyday life. MacDonald sees fear as something
which can come between the would-be believer and
God, as Irene's misadventure with the goblin's creature,
just at the point when she is about to ascend to the
attic, shows. The pattern of events at this point, with
the creature appearing just at that moment, suggests, of
course, that fear and doubt, or inability to fully believe,
are to be equated. Conversely, Curdie's confidence that,
in the upper regions at least, one need only be unafraid
of the goblins not to be vulnerable to them, suggests
that sheer courage and faith are equivalents.

The terrible region of mines and caverns below the
castle, therefore, stands for the state of being cut off
from God because one is immersed in a materialistic
outlook (a state which one ought to fear and of which
the Christ within us is afraid) and is also the state of
being cut off from God *because* one is afraid. The
goblins, in turn, are both an embodiment of one's fears
(whatever those may be) and also symbols of the
fearsome danger represented by the worldly-minded, of
whom MacDonald, like many another Victorian sage,
was only too aware. The climax of the story comes
when the goblins break into the castle and swarm all
over it. They attempt to make off with Irene, but it is
their sheer presence in the dwelling which is a horror
and a contamination. The image lurking behind

MacDonald's rendering of this is clearly that of vermin: they are like rats, and it is as proverbial drowned rats that they end, in the flooded caverns and castle. Throughout MacDonald's writings, the image of rats is used as an incarnation of the fears which can beset the youthful and sensitive. When, in *Ranald Bannerman's Boyhood*, Ranald attempts to pursue an adventure at dead of night, his fears focus on rats (chapters 22–24). More memorably still, the child Annie Anderson finds her initial suffering in the Bruce household come to a head when she is sent upstairs in the dark where she feels vulnerable to rats. Her fears at this point are the culmination of all her fears in her new environment. (Especially interesting is, once again, the association of rats with an outlook of gross materialism and selfishness: the Bruces are clearly an early version of the goblin king and queen.) Rats, therefore, are both an embodiment of the causes of fear and also represent fear itself, threatening and hampering one's contentment and security of mind.

For most of *The Princess and the Goblin*, the goblins do not do very much: they are a source of unease simply because they are there, and the exact form of the threat they represent is not spelt out. They are initially described as makers of mischief; they wish to 'annoy', to 'torment', to 'devise trouble for their neighbours'. Their mere existence is enough to do this, and the trouble they cause, until the end when they try to capture Irene and flood the mines, is merely the destruction of the surface-dwellers' sense of security. They destroy the sense of being *at home* — which is why they are the opposites of Irene's grandmother, whose domain is home, as we have seen. What Irene is being protected from, by guards and by restrictions about being out at night, is fear itself. The story is of her exposure to that emotion, and of her being equipped to meet it.

At the Back of the North Wind deals with an even more

fundamental potential stumbling-block to the Christian believer than even fear or the difficulty of belief: it is about dying. It is the story of a dying child. Despite his apparent vitality, Young Diamond is a victim of poor living conditions which expose him to the cold which kills him. The lovely, motherly, but enigmatic North Wind, with whom he is so happy, is a complex figure standing for many things: she is an embodiment of nature and nature's power, she suggests the caring, motherly spirit within creation, and at times she seems akin to poetic inspiration. She is also what men often call fate, or bad fortune, or ruin, and she is a medium through which God's purpose is achieved, even when that purpose seems to involve death and disaster, as in the sinking of the ship with the loss of many lives and fortunes. All these things, however, are eventually seen as merged in one overriding identification, for men 'have another name for me which they think the most dreadful of all'. (ABNW, p. 386)

Death, of course, is frequently touched upon throughout MacDonald's works and is always more or less positively, even favourably, viewed, although the associated sadness is always acknowledged. Mossy's taste of death in the bath of the Old Man of the Sea, in 'The Golden Key', is usually cited: Mossy pronounces death to be good, and is told that it is not better than life but, rather, is 'only more life'. In the novels, however, it is inevitable that death is presented from the point of view of bereavement, so that it is always a sad landmark. In *At the Back of the North Wind*, however, the reality of what is happening to Diamond is only very occasionally, and indirectly, glimpsed (as when his mother is described as being anxious about his state of health) and the positive side of his fate is given priority. Thus, his near-death while in Sandwich is presented as an opportunity for a marvellous journey, and the moment when he pitches out of the land of the living and into that of the dead is the moment of perhaps the most memorable encounter with North Wind. Even the open windows which kill him (the knot-hole in the thin partition at the beginning; the open bedroom window by which he waits for North Wind for the last time) are made to seem natural and positive things, with scarcely a hint of the danger which, from the mortal perspective, they represent. All North Wind's visits, in fact, are stages by which his health is steadily undermined. This is why Diamond 'must come for all that' (ABNW, p. 58): the opportunities to go with North Wind are understandably welcomed by Diamond, but just occasionally an underlying compulsion is to be glimpsed. Diamond must submit to the North Wind of death taking him away, just as those on the doomed ship have no choice in their cruel-seeming fate — and just as North Wind herself has no choice but bring about such devastation. This work is perhaps MacDonald's most drastic attempt to transform our vision of death, and to offer it as something to be wholeheartedly accepted, despite understandable mortal doubts.

Sleight-of-hand is needed to achieve this, however. Towards the end of the book, Diamond is gradually detached from his family, when they all move to Mr. Raymond's 'small place in Kent' along with Nanny and Jim, the two street arabs whom Diamond has befriended. Within this larger family, Diamond is increasingly the eccentric, other-worldly odd man out. He is taken into service in the house itself, away from his parents, with never a backward look at them. MacDonald carefully organises a backward look, however, at his old home, the scene of the bulk of the book: it has changed somewhat, but not so much as Diamond's new, uncaring attitude towards it has: 'I thought I liked the place so much ... but I find I don't care about it' (ABNW, p. 396). The ordinary sense of rupture with beloved people and places which death usually entails has been muted to nothing, here, and the effect is heightened by bringing forward the narrator, hitherto transparent, as an observing character within the tale. When death finally comes to Diamond, it is a painless, desirable transition.

At the Back of the North Wind is a more unequal work than the *Princess* books, not because it is partially dream-fantasy and partially a realistic novel with a social conscience, but because it is simply too long for its basic matter and consequently suffers from padding. Each *Princess* book has a natural narrative to tell, but the heart of *At the Back of the North Wind* is simply a marvellous, static idea: North Wind herself as an image and as a compendium of all the many and contradictory meanings which we detect in her. As a result, MacDonald has to ceaselessly invent, and draw on source-material as diverse as nursery rhymes, Scots ballads, and his own disastrous northern cruise on the yacht *Blue Bell* earlier in 1869 when he had experienced, painfully and dangerously, the ferocity of illness to a degree which was new to him. The result is lacking in organic unity, as it veers from obvious moralistic allegory to realistic assaults on his reader's social awareness, from embarrassing dream-fables to weak attempts to revise and develop traditional nursery rhymes. Yet no reader would willingly forget the great passages of Diamond's experiences with North Wind: in them, MacDonald displays an inspired invention, combining visual and physical description with a profound, even severe, seriousness which is awe-inspiring. At the end, the work is in danger of making light of death, but in those moments when Diamond encounters North Wind at her most austere and enigmatic, there is no such danger.

There seems a curious discrepancy between writing books for children and writing with a focus on issues which are particularly troubling and difficult to come to terms with. Yet MacDonald's finest children's writing does seem to contain what is especially deep in him: his best non-fantasy work for young people, for example, *Ranald Bannerman's Boyhood*, has a wealth of autobiographical memories of Huntly that is equalled, in his output, only by *Alec Forbes of Howglen*. It avowedly sets out to describe a childhood, and to end when that childhood ends. 'Youth' eventually comes to Ranald when he realises that he is not yet 'a man'. And the touchstone which reveals these successive stages is death: Ranald (like MacDonald) loses his mother at an early age, but throughout the book he is essentially untouched by the loss until he returns from university to discover not only that his playmate Elsie Duff has died but that his friend Turkey had been engaged to her and is therefore sustaining a loss far beyond anything Ranald's life has yet challenged him with. Manhood comes, it seems, when one has faced up to death in the loss of loved ones. The essence of childhood, therefore, is that that challenge is unknown.

To MacDonald, therefore, an important part of the symbolic import of childhood is the absence of fear, or 'rats': childhood is a state of freedom from the anguish which plagues adults, which is why the subjection of children to terrors such as those which blight Annie Anderson's early years in Glamerton is such pollution. It can be difficult, however, to remain innocent of the heartache and the thousand natural shocks that flesh is heir to. As we have seen, childhood stands, in MacDonald's mind, for mankind at its most vulnerable, whether it is being threatened by the Liliths, or the rats, of creation. In the works examined here, it is as if MacDonald has been fending off his own rats, preserving the child in himself and his readers. Greville recalls how 'my father had a wonderful way of catching rats with his hand, thickly gloved' (GMDW, p. 327n).

In these stories, in which mental rats are being caught, it is as if the conventions of writing for children, with their assurance of a happy outcome, and the control of the prominent narrator with his intimate, reliable adult voice, are being used as a thick glove. Writing of such matters for children gave MacDonald the secure stance he needed in order to contemplate difficulties and to reassure himself, once again, that it would be all right in the end.

NOTES

1. George MacDonald, *Unspoken Sermons*, Series 1, London, 1867, pp. 1–26.
2. Roger Lancelyn Green & Walter Hooper, *C. S. Lewis: A Biography*, London, 1974, p. 236.
3. Jacqueline Rose, *The Case of Peter Pan, or The Impossibility of Children's Fiction*, London, 1984, p. 5.
4. Marion Lochhead, *The Renaissance of Wonder in Children's Literature*, Edinburgh, 1977, pp. 32–33.
5. Robert Lee Wolff, *The Golden Key: A Study of the Fiction of George MacDonald*, New Haven, 1961, p. 179.
6. Tony Tanner, 'Mountains and Depths — An Approach to Nineteenth-Century Dualism' in *A Review of English Literature*, 3, 4, October 1962, pp. 51–54.
7. Walter E. Houghton, *The Victorian Frame of Mind, 1830–1870*, New Haven & London, 1957, pp. 54–89.

CHAPTER 6

REPUTATION

At no stage has MacDonald ever been universally held in high repute: he has always appealed to a minority, though the size and scope of that group has varied enormously since he first became prominent in the 1860s. Like many another Victorian novelist of the second rank, he achieved a reputation and a volume of sales which raised him to literary prominence for a time, only to have that position dwindle during the 1880s as public taste passed him by. Even in his heyday, his writing was valued as much for its 'message' — which, for many, was a concept hard to distinguish from a sense of the author's personality — as it was for any narrowly literary qualities it may have had. Nor did the peak of his popularity outlast his own lifetime. Greville MacDonald recalled how he suddenly realised, in the closing years of the century, that his father's work was losing its popular appeal.[1] In fact, it is to be doubted whether MacDonald was ever universally popular: contemporary reviews frequently welcome the moral elevation and the idealism of his approach, but just as frequently describe his work as containing weaknesses as great as its strengths. The persistence of his impenetrable Scots vernacular aroused near-universal bafflement and frustration. To the Victorians he was regarded as a writer of uneven achievement and as having an appeal only to the discerning.

In his lifetime, he was known as a poet and preacher, as well as a writer of prose fiction. It was not long, however, before his reputation dwindled to that of a regional novelist. Within his own lifetime he had begun to drop out of accounts of the development of the novel, and even in a work of specifically Scottish concern, J. H. Millar's *A Literary History of Scotland*, published in 1903 (two years before MacDonald's death) his writing was offered as a curate's egg with his humorous realism praised at the expense of his didacticism, his sense of structure, and his love of symbolism.[2] To Miller, *Phantastes* and *Lilith* were 'tedious and unintelligible' (p. 617), and anecdotal information, over the years, suggests to me that Millar's limited preference for certain of his Scottish stories was echoed by many Scottish readers in the early decades of this century — readers whose love of Scotland was more pronounced than their desire to be in the fashion. The centenary of his birth, in 1924, brought some renewed revival of interest in him — thanks mainly (and justifiably) to Greville's magnificent biography, though MacDonald's old university of Aberdeen did his memory good service with J. M. Bulloch's bibliography, and Grierson's sane, balanced assessment in *The Aberdeen University Review*.

Grierson makes it clear that MacDonald has to be approached, if at all, as a preacher: the ordinary reader cannot just pick him up and expect to be entertained as by other writers. This is a conclusion which much of the history of MacDonald's reputation in the twentieth century seems to bear out. The current growth of interest in, and respect for, his work seems mainly to derive from his appeal to that combination of tastes perhaps best embodied in C. S. Lewis. Lewis was an enthusiast, as is well known, from the moment in February 1916 when he stumbled on *Phantastes* on a station bookstall, and his advocacy — most widely broadcast by his 1946 essay of introduction to his anthology of extracts from MacDonald's writing — has been decisive in establishing the author as a valuable Christian thinker and as a myth-maker. Lewis's assessment that MacDonald's claim on us is that of the fantasy writing rather than that of the novels is also now the standard view.

It was also the view of the writer who, along with Lewis, laid the foundations for the current growth of awareness of MacDonald. Robert Lee Wolff's *The Golden Key* (1961) gave MacDonald a new interest in the eyes of many, thanks to the book's enthusiastic Freudianism which used the writing as psychoanalytic evidence for a more complex and disturbing picture of MacDonald's psyche than had prevailed hitherto. This book set a further pattern, in that it was the first sign that most of the modern discussion of MacDonald would come from North America rather than Great Britain, as several later books, and a growing academic industry, have testified. This fact, along with the advocacy and discipleship of Christian Romantics like Lewis and Tolkien, has hindered the reassessment of MacDonald's Scottish writing.

Much has been achieved in the academic revival of interest in Scottish literature in recent decades, but MacDonald has benefited scarcely at all: he is not much better known to Scottish readers or critics than he was in 1960. His ultimate place is not yet decided, and his location on the scale between oblivion and universal acclaim is still to seek. If his rediscovery has been welcomed by twentieth-century Christians, and if it is equally clear that he will never again attain the prominence in the minds of English-speaking readers that he enjoyed in the 1860s and 1870s, it still seems necessary to try to assess him in the Scottish context. Scottish critics have still to grapple with his fantasy works and works for children — becoming familiar with them and relating them to the longer reaches of Scottish writing. Similarly, the strengths and weaknesses of the Scottish novels need to become at least more widely known. Were that to happen, our sense of the complexity of Scottish fiction would be enriched, even if it be ultimately decided that they have less to offer the modern reader than they had to his contemporaries. Furthermore, as MacDonald is a writer who particularly benefits from being read in bulk, the understanding of that narrow range of his writing which the twentieth century appears to have taken to its heart would be immeasurably increased.

NOTES

1. Greville MacDonald, *Reminiscences of a Specialist*, London, 1932, p. 330.
2. J. H. Millar, *A Literary History of Scotland*, London, 1903, p. 617.

SELECT BIBLIOGRAPHY

Works by MacDonald

A Book of Strife, in the form of The Diary of an Old Soul (London, 1880).

A Dish of Orts (London, 1893).

Alec Forbes of Howglen (London, 1865).

At the Back of the North Wind (London, 1871; rpt. New York, 1950).

Castle Warlock (London, 1882).

David Elginbrod (London, 1863).

Donal Grant (London, 1883).

The Elect Lady (London, 1888).

England's Antiphon (London, 1874).

Heather and Snow (London, 1893).

Lilith: A Romance (London, 1895; rpt., with *Phantastes*, and intro. by C. S. Lewis, London, 1962).

Malcolm (London, 1875).

The Marquis of Lossie (London, 1877).

Paul Faber, Surgeon (London, 1879).

Phantastes: A Faerie Romance for Men and Women (London, 1858; rpt. in Everyman's Library, London, 1915; rpt. with *Lilith*, and intro. by C. S. Lewis, London, 1962; rpt. as Everyman Paperback with intro. by David Holbrook, London, 1983).

Poetical Works, 2 vols. (London, 1893).

The Princess and Curdie (London, 1883; rpt. Harmondsworth, 1966).

The Princess and the Goblin (London, 1872; rpt. Harmondsworth, 1964).

Ranald Bannerman's Boyhood (London, 1871; rpt. London & Glasgow, 1911).

Robert Falconer (London, 1868).
Salted With Fire: A Tale (London, 1897).
Sir Gibbie (London, 1879).
Unspoken Sermons, 3 sers. (London, 1867, 1885, 1889).
What's Mine's Mine (London, 1886).
Wilfred Cumbermede (London, 1872).
Works of Fancy and Imagination, 10 vols. (London, 1871).

In recent years, there have appeared in American paperback editions heavily abbreviated versions of MacDonald's realistic novels under such titles as *The Tutor's First Love* [*David Elginbrod*] and *The Maiden's Bequest* [*Alec Forbes of Howglen*]. Needless to say, these have no value to the serious reader of MacDonald.

Bibliography

J. M. Bulloch, *A Centennial Bibliography of George MacDonald* (Aberdeen, 1925).

Biographical Studies

Greville MacDonald, *George MacDonald and his Wife* (London, 1924).
Greville MacDonald, *Reminiscences of a Specialist* (London, 1932).
Ronald MacDonald, 'George MacDonald: A Personal Note' in *From a Northern Window*, ed. Frederick Watson (London, 1911), pp. 55–113.
David S. Robb, 'George MacDonald at Blackfriars Chapel' in *North Wind: Journal of the George MacDonald Society*, 5, 1986, pp. 3–20.

As this book goes to press, there is word of a new biographical and critical study of MacDonald by William Raeper.

Books on MacDonald

Robert Lee Wolff, *The Golden Key: A Study of the Fiction of George MacDonald* (New Haven, 1961).

Richard H. Reis, *George MacDonald*, Twayne's English Authors Series 119 (New York, 1972).

Rolland Hein, *The Harmony Within: The Spiritual Vision of George MacDonald* (Grand Rapids, 1982).

Shorter Studies

H. J. C. Grierson, 'George MacDonald' in *The Aberdeen University Review*, 12 (1924–1925), no. 34, November 1924, pp. 1–13.

David Holbrook, Introduction to *Phantastes* (London, 1983), pp. vii–xxv.

C. S. Lewis, Preface to *George MacDonald: An Anthology* (London, 1946), pp. 10–22.

Colin N. Manlove, *Modern Fantasy: Five Studies* (Cambridge, 1975), pp. 55–98.

Colin N. Manlove, 'George MacDonald's Early Scottish Novels' in *Nineteenth-Century Scottish Fiction: Critical Essays*, ed. Ian M. Campbell (Manchester, 1979), pp. 68–88.

Colin N. Manlove, *The Impulse of Fantasy Literature* (London, 1983), pp. 70–92.

Roderick F. McGillis, 'George MacDonald—The *Lilith* Manuscripts', *Scottish Literary Journal*, 4, 2, December 1977, pp. 40–57.

Roderick F. McGillis, 'George MacDonald and the Lilith Legend in the Nineteenth Century', *Mythlore*, 6, 1979, pp. 3–11.

Stephen Prickett, *Romanticism and Religion: The Tradition of Coleridge and Wordsworth in the Victorian Church* (Cambridge, 1976), pp. 211–248.

Stephen Prickett, *Victorian Fantasy* (Hassocks, 1979), pp. 150–197.

David S. Robb, 'George MacDonald's Aberdeenshire Fairytale' in *Studies in Scottish Fiction: Nineteenth Century*, Scottish Studies, Publications of the Scottish Studies Centre of the Johannes Gutenberg Universitat Mainz in Germersheim, 3, eds. H. W. Drescher and J. Schwend (Frankfurt am Main, Bern, New York, 1985), pp. 205–216.

See also my forthcoming article, 'George MacDonald and Animal Magnetism', in *Seven: An Anglo-American Literary Review*, 8, 1987.